BUSES
YEARBOOK 2014

Edited by STEWART J. BROWN

KEY PUBLISHING

BUSES
YEARBOOK 2014
First Published August 2013

ISBN: 978-0-946219-31-5

© Key Publishing Ltd 2013

Published by Key Publishing Ltd.
www.keypublishing.com

Printed in England by Berforts Information Press Ltd, Southfield Road, Eynsham, Oxford, OX29 4JB.

FSC
www.fsc.org
MIX
Paper from responsible sources
FSC® C013262

FRONT COVER: **The most common double-deck type in the East Yorkshire fleet is the Wright Eclipse Gemini on Volvo B7TL, and later B9TL, chassis. (see page 104).**

BACK COVER (UPPER): **Bradford Corporation 735 (DKY 735), a 1945 Karrier W, was rebodied by East Lancs in 1959 with this forward entrance body as part of the Bradford fleet's modernisation. (see page 18).**

BACK COVER (LOWER): **The final 60 chassis of GMT's last Leyland Atlantean order, which would have taken the fleet numbers for PTE standards up to 8825, was cancelled and replaced by one for 60 Olympians. The first 25 of these started to arrive at the end of 1982 and featured Leyland's automatic Hydracyclic gearbox. (see page 60).**

PREVIOUS PAGE:
The opening of the M1 in 1959 prompted Midland Red to develop its high-speed C5 coach, reputed to be capable of 85mph, for the Birmingham-London service. (see page 48).

CONTENTS

50th EDITION

Selnec PTE operated this ex-Leigh Corporation AEC Regent III with lowbridge East Lancs body. It has been renumbered by Selnec and carries Selnec advertising, but the blue Leigh livery would be retained by this bus until its withdrawal. (see page 76)

50 YEARS
of *Buses Yearbook*

Buses Yearbook marks 50 years of publication with this, the 2014 edition. It started out as *Buses Annual* in 1964, and was re-titled *Buses Yearbook* in 1989. Four editions – from 1968 to 1971 – were simply titled *Buses*.

1964: The start of it all: the first *Buses Annual*.

The first editor was R A Smith – Robin Alan Smith – who worked in the public relations department at London Transport. He edited the first four Annuals, and was succeeded for *Buses sixty-eight* (as it was styled) by G W Watts. Gordon Watts was well-known as the compiler of vehicle news for *Buses Illustrated*, and was a personnel officer for HM Customs & Excise.

Major change came in 1972 when Gavin Booth took over and the *Buses Annual* title reappeared. Under both Robin Alan Smith and Gordon Watts, there had been a relatively small number of lengthy articles. Gavin introduced the format which has continued with little change since, mixing longer articles with photofeatures and other shorter items, giving readers much more variety. Gavin worked for the Scottish Bus Group, but was also a respected transport journalist. I took over from Gavin in 1987, just as I started a career change as a full-time freelance writer and marketing consultant.

The first *Buses Annual* contained 11 articles in its 96 pages, by writers who were well-known at that time, including Alan Townsin, the highly-respected editor of *Buses Illustrated* from 1959 to 1965. In 1966 there were just eight features, with Alan Townsin again appearing alongside, among others, John F Parke, who had taken over the editorship of *Buses Illustrated*. That

issue had 90 photographs, all black-and-white, as was normal at the time.

The revamped 1972 *Buses Annual* was bigger – 132 pages – and contained no fewer than 24 items. It was also the first to feature colour photographs inside. I made my first appearance as a contributor in that edition, as did Robert Jowitt, whose elegant prose and sometimes controversial approach is still entertaining readers four decades letter. He is not the longest-standing regular contributor. That distinction goes to Colchester-based photographer Geoff Mills, who first appeared in the 1967 edition.

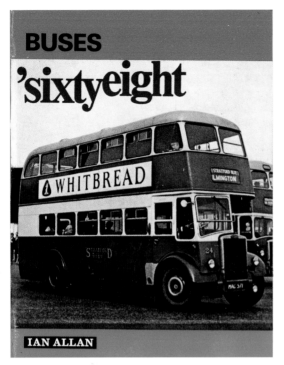

BUSES 'sixtyeight

IAN ALLAN

1968: Gordon Watts takes over and "Annual" is dropped from the title.

BUSES ANNUAL £1·50

Edited by Gavin Booth

CITY CENTRE

1972: New look, new editor: the first Annual under Gavin Booth's editorship.

BUSES YEAR BOOK

Edited by Stewart J. Brown

1989: New name: the first *Buses Yearbook*.

Stephen Morris, who succeeded John Parke as editor of *Buses*, has contributed to the Yearbook from time to time, while present *Buses* editor Alan Millar first appeared in the 1978 edition, missed out in 1979, and has been in every volume since 1980.

Over the course of 50 years *Buses Yearbook* has attracted contributions from a wide range of talented writers and photographers. And, of course, without the support of these contributors there would be no Yearbook. The job of each of the editors over the years has been the same. To find material which will appeal to a broad spectrum of readers in terms of vehicle types, of geography, and of period. Too much on, say, the pre-deregulation era, might not appeal to readers whose interests lie in more recent times. And the converse is true, too – and I am aware that many readers of *Buses Yearbook* have been loyal supporters over a long number of years.

So, in welcoming you to this milestone edition, the second to be produced under the stewardship of Key Publishing who took over *Buses* magazine and the Yearbook from Ian Allan in 2012, let me thank both you, the readers, and those willing contributors who have over the years entertained and informed you.

Stewart J. Brown

Externally, the first batches of Volvo Olympians differed little from their Leyland predecessors, except for the rectangular headlamps and the discreet Volvo and Alexander badges under them. This is a 1994 delivery; this batch had the shortest lives in Lothian service, just 12-13 years. GAVIN BOOTH

Lothian's Olympian legacy

Edinburgh is at times described as the Athens of the North. **GAVIN BOOTH** looks at the history of an apt model for the city, the Olympians operated by Lothian.

Coming on the heels of 588 Atlanteans, not to mention 452 Titan PDs before them, Leyland must have been hoping that Lothian Region Transport would remain faithful and plump for its new Olympian at the start of the 1980s. Poor old Leyland had misjudged the double-deck market by assuming that its sophisticated Titan TN15 would be the model bus operators would be queuing up to buy. When bus companies let Leyland know that the Titan was definitely *not* what they wanted, Leyland turned to the designers at its Bristol factory to come up with something operators *would* buy, and project B45 was developed, morphing into the Olympian.

Lothian was a target customer for Leyland and had been convinced to order two Titan TN15s in the early days of that model. Labour problems dogged the Titan's progress – it was first built at the Park Royal coachworks in London, then moved to Leyland's

Workington plant, not before AEC at Southall and ECW at Lowestoft had been considered as possible homes.

All of the uncertainty led several of the operators who had placed orders for trial batches of Titans to cancel these orders. Lothian was one of these and its two Titans eventually materialised as its first two Olympians. These were early chassis (numbers ON42/43) and had bodywork by Lothian's then-favoured builder, Walter Alexander at Falkirk.

As numbers 666 and 667 they entered Lothian service in April 1982. They were 9.6m-long buses with two-door Alexander RH bodies, which were broadly similar in configuration to the last Atlanteans that preceded them by just five months.

But not before Lothian had considered at least one of the rival double-deck models that had appeared to challenge Leyland's market domination. Unease about Leyland's position had led to the development of competing models like the Dennis Dominator, MCW Metrobus and Volvo Ailsa and Lothian had tried an Ailsa in 1976 and in 1981 borrowed a Reading Transport MCW Metrobus to test in service. The Metrobus was probably the greatest threat to Leyland, but Lothian resisted its charms and bought only Olympians for the next 15 years.

The two 9.6m Alexander-bodied Olympians were to remain unique in the Lothian fleet, as all subsequent Olympians bought new were longer buses and – horror of horrors – the next examples didn't even have Alexander bodies; the last time Lothian and its predecessor, Edinburgh Corporation Transport, had bought double-deck bus bodies from 'down south' was in 1957, the last of a big batch of Metro-Cammell-bodied PD2s.

But Leyland was working hard to convince its customers of the advantages of one-stop shopping. If arch-rivals MCW could promote the benefits of dealing with a single supplier to sell its buses, so could Leyland. And many customers still had bitter memories of the chaos that reigned in the early 1970s when, as a result of the UK's economic and labour problems, the supply of bus chassis and bodies got hopelessly out of synch – in some cases customers had to wait years to get deliveries.

Leyland had its in-house bodybuilders, Eastern Coach Works at Lowestoft and Roe at Leeds. Buy your Olympians with ECW or Roe bodies, customers were told, and we can guarantee delivery dates. No doubt there was a financial incentive too, which would help explain why not only Lothian but Scottish Bus Group and Greater Glasgow PTE were lured away from Alexander at Falkirk to ECW – and also to Roe at the

The first two Lothian Leyland Olympians differed from subsequent deliveries as they were just 9.6m long. They had Alexander RH-type bodies. This one is seen in 1999. It is now preserved. GAVIN BOOTH

Lothian's long ECW Olympians were impressive-looking buses, and gave good service for up to 19 years. This 1983 delivery is seen in Edinburgh's Princes Street in 1996; it would last in service until 2000. GAVIN BOOTH

The rounder lines of the ECW-bodied bus contrast with the more angular style of the Alexander RH-type following it up The Mound in Edinburgh in 1995 past the National Gallery of Scotland.
GAVIN BOOTH

The ECW Olympians were largely replaced by Plaxton President-bodied Dennis Tridents. This is a 2002 photograph. GAVIN BOOTH

PTE. The people at Alexander were understandably upset.

Lothian wanted bigger buses; its Atlanteans had been mostly 75-seaters but it was looking for more capacity. It borrowed a 10-metre Preston Corporation Atlantean with two-door Alexander body in 1981 and used it successfully in service in Edinburgh. So its first batch of Olympians was specified as 35 10.3m-long models with ECW 81-seat bodies.

These started to arrive in November 1982 and delivery was complete by February 1983, so Leyland kept its end of the bargain on delivery times. The ECW body style for the Olympian was a classic of its time, and it looked even more impressive to the 10.3m length of the Lothian buses, with an extra short-length window bay amidships. Most contemporary ECW Olympians were 9.6m long, and although there were some early long Olympians for Hong Kong operators with low-height bodies, long left-hand drive demonstrators for Athens, Baghdad and Lisbon, and 19 more production models for Athens, the Lothian buses remained unique in home market sales. The nearest equivalent was a single 10.3m Olympian/ECW with just one door for Preston in 1984; this bus was initially used as a Leyland demonstrator.

The second batch of ECW Olympians came in October/November 1983 – 34 two-door buses with 83 seats, with the staircase opposite the exit door, rather than behind the driver's cab, and this became the standard layout for future deliveries from ECW.

The Olympian deliveries allowed Lothian to replace its older Leyland Atlanteans and a further batch of 34 ECW Olympians arrived between October and December 1984. The last bus in the batch, 770, was retained by Leyland as a demonstrator and was shown at the UITP exhibition at Brussels in May 1985. It returned to Lothian, where it was used in service for a few weeks before being bought back by Leyland. It was converted by ECW to a demonstrator for Thailand, where Leyland hoped to win large orders, and eventually ended up in service with Citybus in Hong Kong.

A second 770 was included in Lothian's 1985 Olympians, 25 delivered in December 1985 and January 1986, by which time the plant at Lowestoft was living on borrowed time and in the summer of 1986 it was announced that ECW would close following the completion of an order for 260 Olympians for London Buses.

After 128 ECW-bodied Olympians, Lothian had to find a new body supplier. It turned back to Alexander, which was still smarting after the switch to ECW, and

ABOVE: **Not all of the Olympians transferred to Lothian's tour fleet were open-toppers – not immediately, at any rate. This 1988 Olympian in City Sightseeing branding in Princes Street in 2004 was later converted to open-top layout. The Mercedes-Benz minibus on the right is operating on the innovative Edinburgh-Dunfermline taxibus service introduced experimentally by Stagecoach.** GAVIN BOOTH

BELOW: **In 2002-2004 Lothian transferred eight Olympians to its driver training fleet. TB322 of 1988 is seen in 2006; following its withdrawal from these duties it has been restored by Lothian Buses to its original condition as bus 322.** GAVIN BOOTH

had raised questions at the highest level about the Scottish capital buying bus bodies built in England.

With deregulation and privatisation affecting the market for new full-size buses, Alexander was more than happy to rebuild its relationship with Lothian, and would go on to body all of Lothian's future Olympians.

The first batch of 36 came in 1988, 10.3m Olympians with RH type 81-seat bodies, a substantial order at a time when few operators were buying new double-deckers. The RH bodies were similar in outline to Lothian's two original Olympians, but had deep vee windscreens and a lower panel styling that was to remain unique to Lothian. Where previous Lothian Olympians had Leyland TL11 engines, the new Alexander-bodied ones had the now-standard Cummins L10 unit. These were followed by 36 more in 1989, including six single-door coach-seated 78-seaters for tour and airport work. More two-door 81-seaters followed – 36 in 1990, another 36 in 1991 and a further 22 in 1992-93. These would be Lothian's last *Leyland* Olympians, following Volvo's acquisition of Leyland Bus in 1988 and its decision to revamp the model as a Volvo in 1993. The Olympian name was retained – the only Volvo with a name rather

Lothian's Alexander Royale-bodied Volvo Olympians were handsome buses. This 1996 example is seen in 2008.

A 1983 Olympian/Roe, new to London Country, working for Lothian's Edinburgh Tour in 2007, five years after its acquisition with the Guide Friday business in Edinburgh. GAVIN BOOTH

than letters and numbers – and the Volvo THD102KF engine was offered as well as the Cummins L10 – again it was rare for Volvo to offer a proprietary unit.

Lothian had moved to the Cummins L10 in 1988 and stuck with this for its first *Volvo* Olympian deliveries in 1994, when it took 34 with the usual Alexander RH type 81-seat bodies. Another 33 similar buses followed in 1995. Lothian was interested in the new more powerful Cummins M11 engine as an alternative to the existing L10; Volvo said it couldn't be fitted to the Olympian, but Lothian fitted an M11 in bus 964, which was by all accounts a flying machine; it even had notices in the cab reminding drivers of its extra power. It had its M11 to the end of its Lothian days.

Now Lothian was ready to upgrade its Olympian specification and all subsequent examples had Volvo engines and Alexander's more rounded Royale variation of the RH-type structure. There would be 33 of these in 1996, all but three being two-door 81- or 80-seaters; the other three were single-door 76-seaters with coach seats for tours and airport duties. The different seating capacity of the two-door buses is explained by the decision to sample modular seating on 10 buses, and it was difficult to squeeze

Two of the coach-seated one-door Royale Olympians ended their lives on normal bus duties, and were repainted in this brighter red/white livery for the lengthy 15 route, as seen in Portobello in 2009 with a similar First Scotland East bus behind. GAVIN BOOTH

more than 80 seats in. Lothian's last new Olympians were 34 delivered in 1997, all two-door 81-seat buses.

There is a widely-held belief that the Royale Olympians were the best step-entrance double-deckers Lothian had ever had, offering a quality of ride, comfort and performance that their successors struggled to achieve.

But these were not Lothian's last Olympians. The growth of the tour business in Edinburgh led to

The Guide Friday acquisition brought several older Olympians into the Lothian fleet, like this 1984 ex-Cardiff Bus East Lancs-bodied example in Edinburgh Tour livery in 2002. GAVIN BOOTH

Lothian acquiring two competitors in 2002, Guide Friday and Mac Tours, and the Guide Friday fleet included a rag-bag of buses including nine elderly open-top Olympians, all with Gardner 6LXB engines; four were ex-Cardiff with East Lancs bodies, another four ex-London Country with Roe bodies, and there was an ex-Yorkshire Rider bus with rare Optare bodywork. One of the Cardiff buses was new in 1981 with chassis number ON44, following on from Lothian's two pilot Olympians. Some of the ex-Guide Friday Olympians were sold fairly soon, but others managed a few summers in Edinburgh before they went – like their brothers - for further open-top service; some ended up working overseas.

The ex-Guide Friday Olympians joined Olympians from the main Lothian fleet that had been converted to open-top and part-open-top layouts for tour work, replacing older Atlanteans. No ECW-bodied Olympians were converted, but from 1999 buses from the 1988 Alexander-bodied batch were converted, some for the Oxford Classic Tour in 2000, in which Lothian was a partner; the Oxford buses returned to Edinburgh in 2002. Initially Lothian's open-top Olympians were in a predominantly white livery, but from 2001 appeared in the red City Sightseeing colours. Later conversions were allocated to other Lothian open-top brands – the green/cream Edinburgh Tour (the former Guide

Lothian had ordered two Leyland Titan TN15 models, which were allocated fleet numbers 599/600. The order was cancelled and the two original Olympians were their replacements, but Keith McGillivray has imagined how the Titans would have looked if they had been built. KEITH MCGILLIVRAY

Friday operation), and blue/yellow Majestic Tour. There were also closed-top Olympians liveried for the tour operations; some were subsequently converted to open-top, while others retained their roofs.

Normal withdrawals of Lothian's closed-top Olympians started in 2000, when the first of the ECWs were sold, and all of these had been withdrawn by 2004. The first Alexander-bodied Olympians went in 2004 and the very last went in August 2009, with a good allocation on the 23 route on the last day, with front boards – 'tram boards' in Lothian-speak – proclaiming 'Last day of traditional step entrance buses'. The last *Leyland* Olympians had been withdrawn in March 2009 with a similar flourish, and tram boards reading 'Leyland 1919-2009 Final day in Edinburgh'. Lothian's reputation for high maintenance standards meant that operators were queuing up to buy the Olympians; with 80-plus seats – and more if you removed the centre exit door – they were ideal for service and schools work.

The tour Olympians lasted a bit longer, with sales between 2008 and 2011, and most found ready buyers in the UK and overseas. They were replaced by new and converted Dennis Tridents from the main fleet, as were eight Olympians transferred from 2002 to Lothian's driver training fleet and withdrawn in 2009 and 2012.

The Olympian – built at Bristol, Workington and Irvine in a production life just short of 20 years – could well have enjoyed a longer life but for the move towards low-floor double-deckers. Volvo's first foray into this field was a concept vehicle that became the B7L chassis, but operators were unhappy about the long rear overhang and the engine mounted in the rear nearside corner, and Volvo rushed back to the drawing board to come up with the B7TL, with a mechanical layout more acceptable to UK operators.

Lothian had inspected the B7L prototype in Edinburgh but turned to Dennis for its first low-floor double-deckers in 1999, although Volvo managed to get its foot back in the Lothian double-deck door from 2005.

The biggest single customer for the Olympian was Kowloon Motor Bus of Hong Kong, which bought 1,800 Olympians, followed by groups (1,064 for National Bus Company, 993 for Stagecoach); Lothian ended up with the largest number of Olympians in a single UK fleet – its 430 representing 7% of the home market total. And they served Edinburgh and the Lothians well for just short of 30 years.

Lothian has kept two Olympians in its heritage fleet – 1988 Leyland/Alexander RH 322 and 1997 Volvo/Alexander Royale 285, and Leyland/ECW 777 is also preserved locally.

The distinctive two-tone brown and red coaches of Bere Regis & District were synonymous with rural Dorset. For many years Bedfords formed the mainstay of this sizeable fleet, and a typical example is this 1959 Plaxton-bodied SB1. It is pictured leaving Sturminster Newton in November 1982 while working the Blandford Forum to Okeford Fitzpaine service.

Dorset
VARIETY

Mark Bailey looks back at buses in Dorset in the last two decades of the 20th century.

For many years Bournemouth Transport favoured Alexander bodywork for its double-deck fleet. Typical of this period are two Leyland PDR1A/1 Atlanteans dating from 1971 and 1969 and seen in Christchurch in 1985. Bournemouth was the most southerly customer for this style of Alexander body.

Dorset is one of England's southernmost counties, with a coastline stretching from Lyme Regis in the west to Christchurch in the east, and including the Jurassic Coast, a World Heritage Site. Most of the population live in the coastal towns of Bournemouth, Poole, Weymouth, Christchurch, Swanage and Bridport, and in the county town of Dorchester. Inland Dorset is essentially rural with a sprinkling of small towns such as Sherborne, Shaftesbury, Gillingham, Blandford and Wimborne.

At the start of the 1980s the county was served by two NBC subsidies. Western National served the south west, while Hants & Dorset operated in the south east. In 1983, as part of the break up of NBC, these operations passed to Southern National and Wilts & Dorset respectively. The rural remainder of Dorset was served by one of England's largest independents - Bere Regis & District Motor Services - which itself would disappear in the mid 1990s. The county's only municipal operator, Bournemouth Transport, would prove to be the one constant in the period.

With current renewed interest in battery buses, it is worth remembering the technology has been tried before. Bournemouth Transport was an early user, and purchased this Dodge KC60 with 18-seat body by Rootes in 1979. It operated on the Centeride town centre service - where it was photographed in 1985 - until withdrawal in 1987, when it was deemed uneconomical to replace its ageing electric motor.

A batch of 20 Leyland ONLXB/1R Olympians with unusual Marshall bodywork was delivered to Bournemouth Transport in 1982, and were the only Olympians to be bodied by the Cambridge-based bodybuilder. One arrives in Poole in July 1985 on the service from Boscombe.

Left: Comfy Lux was the name used by Pearce, Darch & Willcox, who were based in the village of Cattistock. A small network of services linked rural communities in north-west Dorset with Dorchester, Yeovil and Sherborne. Seen in Dorchester in May 1984 is an elderly Duple-bodied Bedford SB3, awaiting returning shoppers for the service to Sydling St Nicholas. The business was sold in 1990 to the Cawlett group, parent of Southern National.

Right: The cream and red livery of Bournemouth-based Excelsior was a familiar sight throughout the UK for many years. In 1984 the company took delivery of 17 Quest 80 VM models, with Plaxton Paramount 3200 coachwork which featured a distinctive low windscreen. The 'VM' in the chassis designation represented the initials of Excelsior managing director Vernon Maitland. Unfortunately the coaches were blighted by reliability problems and were soon withdrawn.

Left: In 1993 Wilts & Dorset purchased the business of Kimber of Blandford Forum, who traded as Damory Coaches, and resurrected the dormant company name of Hants & Dorset Motor Services to keep the acquisition separate from the main fleet. One of the vehicles transferred from W&D was this Plaxton-bodied Leyland Leopard PSU3C/4R, dating from 1976. It is pictured in Dorchester in 1994 working on the service from Milton Abbas.

Dorset Transit was formed in 1996 by the Cawlett group to circumvent the revocation by the Traffic Commissioner of Southern National's Weymouth to Portland licence, due to overly aggressive competition with rival operator Weybus. A Carlyle-bodied Mercedes-Benz 709D shows the new identity and livery in 1997 as it passes through the village of Easton on the Isle of Portland.

In 1982 Barry's of Weymouth took over the Dorchester town services from Southern National and used the Interbus fleetname for this operation, which lasted until 1987. Interbus vehicles sometimes worked other Barry's routes, as seen here with a former Thames Valley 41-seat ECW-bodied Bristol LH6L of 1969 vintage. It was pictured in Bridport in June 1985, having arrived on the Saturdays-only service from Weymouth.

Maybury's of Cranborne was probably best known for its double-deck sightseeing tours of London, but it did work a few rural services closer to home, mainly to Salisbury in neighbouring Wiltshire. The company had a brief flirtation with urban operations in Dorset, as shown by an ex-West Midlands PTE East Lancs-bodied Daimler Fleetline CRG6LX. It is leaving Bournemouth Square in August 1990 on service 194 to Turlin Moor and Upton, on the northern reaches of Poole Harbour.

Mid Dorset Coaches was the trading name of House, based in the village of Hilton. Pictured just having arrived in Dorchester from Hilton in May 1984 is a Duple Dominant-bodied Ford R1014 which was previously a Ford demonstrator. The business and vehicles were sold to Bere Regis & District in September 1987 on the retirement of the proprietors.

In 1983 Smiths of Portland restarted regular bus operation between the island and Weymouth, and in 1989 the business was acquired by the Cawlett group, parent of Southern National. Pictured in August 1990 leaving Weymouth's King's Statue with a healthy load is an Alexander-bodied Leyland Leopard PSU3F/4R new in 1981 to Central SMT.

In May 1993 competition broke out when Routemaster Bournemouth commenced operating from the former Corporation trolleybus depot in Southcote Road. Very soon three routes and a town tour were being worked by 15 Routemasters and six Atlanteans and Fleetlines. Bournemouth Transport retaliated by introducing a White Buses unit running identical routes. This bus, originally London Transport RM219 but latterly with Clydeside Scottish where it was re-registered, is seen in June 1994 working route 607 from Somerford. Two months later the operation closed down.

Deregulation of local bus services in 1986 prompted NBC coach operator Shamrock & Rambler to introduce a network of services in the Bournemouth, Poole and Christchurch area, initially run by minibuses under the resurrected Charlie's Cars identity. In July 1987 NBC sold the company to the Drawlane group, and full-sized vehicles were subsequently introduced bearing the fleetname S&R Buses. Pictured at Bournemouth Square in 1988 is a 49-seat Leyland National acquired from fellow Drawlane subsidiary Midland Red North. Bus operations ceased in December 1988.

The surviving pair of a batch of six Roe-bodied Daimler Fleetlines that had originally been ordered by Gosport & Fareham (Provincial) but were delivered in 1971 to Hants & Dorset were taken on by Wilts & Dorset when it was its reformed in 1983. They had been relegated to school duties when pictured in June 1985 at Swanage railway station.

Verwood Transport commenced operations in 1981 with services to Poole, Bournemouth and Christchurch. Several double-deckers were operated, including this smart 1966 Northern Counties-bodied Guy Arab V which had been new to Lancashire United Transport. It is seen loading in Christchurch in July 1985, sporting the blue livery based on that of erstwhile Middlesbrough Corporation. The business was sold to Wilts & Dorset in February 1989.

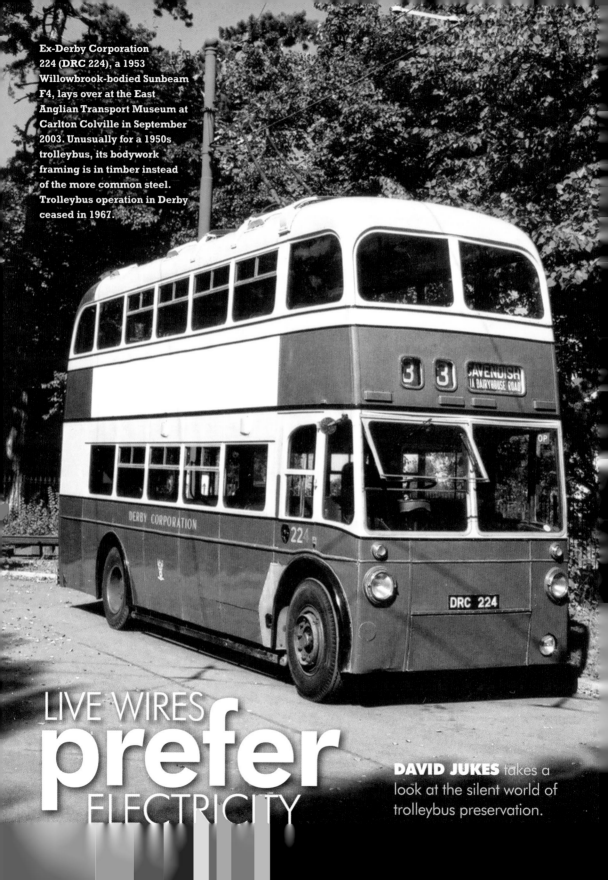

Ex-Derby Corporation 224 (DRC 224), a 1953 Willowbrook-bodied Sunbeam F4, lays over at the East Anglian Transport Museum at Carlton Colville in September 2003. Unusually for a 1950s trolleybus, its bodywork framing is in timber instead of the more common steel. Trolleybus operation in Derby ceased in 1967.

LIVE WIRES
prefer
ELECTRICITY

DAVID JUKES takes a look at the silent world of trolleybus preservation.

'Live wires prefer electricity' is the unique selling proposition applied to the nearside of former Derby Corporation 237, a 1960 Roe-bodied Sunbeam F4A trolleybus. It is a statement that perfectly describes the trolleybus preservationists who between them have secured for posterity over 100 trolleybuses representing some 30 UK undertakings and a dozen or so more from overseas, including repatriated UK exports.

London Transport was the first organisation to preserve a trolleybus in this country when it most wisely set aside the capital's first trolleybus, ex-London United 1, a 1931 UCC-bodied AEC 663T, which was stored at Reigate after its 1948 withdrawal until placed on display at Clapham museum from 1960. Number 1 made a ceremonial run on the last day of London's trolleybuses, 8 May 1962, and has more recently made working visits to the East Anglia Transport Museum at Carlton Colville, near Lowestoft, in 1990 and 2012. In between, it has been displayed at the LT museum in Syon Park and then at Covent Garden and its current home, Acton Depot.

More trolleybuses were later added to the London Transport collection – 260, a 1936 Metro-Cammell-bodied AEC 664T, from 1959 to 1962 when it was replaced by the more original 1253, a 1939 all-Leyland LPTB70. In fact 260 escaped the scrapman at the eleventh hour and was acquired by Tony Belton and Fred Ivey, two of the London Trolleybus Preservation Society's founding members. It was stored in Reading and at LT's Edmonton garage until moved to Carlton Colville in 1986 although was allowed to escape for fund-raising tours of Reading and Bournemouth in 1967 and 1968 respectively.

By comparison, 1253 has led a quieter life and is statically displayed at Covent Garden although it was loaned to the East Anglia Transport Museum in 2006 while the London Transport Museum was being refurbished. Also enjoying a relatively restful retirement is 1768, a 1948 Metro-Cammell-bodied BUT 9641T, which was one of just two of the Q1 class not exported to Spain for further service. It was loaned to the East Anglia Transport Museum from 1992 until 2000 before making a further visit in 2012 alongside Acton Depot stable mate number 1.

London Transport was most fortunate in having somewhere to safely display or store its preserved trolleybuses under cover, both in the short and longer term. For other trolleybus preservationists, life was not to be as easy or straightforward.

The late 1950s and 1960s saw the majority of the UK's trolleybus systems close and their routes converted to motor bus operation – just Cardiff, Walsall, Teesside and Bradford survived into the 1970s with Bradford's and the UK's last trolleybus running on 26 March 1972. The swinging sixties were to see many trolleybuses acquired for preservation as they quickly disappeared from the streets, although some were later recovered from post-service use as

Former Reading Corporation 186 (VRD 186), a 1961 Burlingham-bodied Sunbeam F4A, passed to Teesside Municipal Transport in 1969 where it was numbered 11, and later T291. It was TMT's final trolleybus and is preserved in its decorated condition, commemorating trolleybus operation on Teesside from 1919 to 1971. T291 is seen on static display at the Black Country Living Museum's 2006 Trolleybus Fortnight event – it currently resides at Sandtoft.

Visiting vehicles were often a feature of the Black Country Living Museum's Trolleybus Fortnight gatherings. The then newly restored ex-Belfast Corporation 246 (2206 OI), a 1958 Harkness-bodied Sunbeam F4A, had its unique hydraulic-based braking system returned to full working order using the Museum Transport Group's expertise enabling its appearance at the 2006 event before later returning to its Carlton Colville home.

Resident at the Black Country Living Museum and seen on home ground in June 2006 is ex-Wolverhampton 433 (DUK 833), a 1946 Sunbeam W with 1959 Roe bodywork. The last Wolverhampton trolleybuses operated in 1967.

holiday homes, storage sheds, meeting rooms and suchlike. Others were to return from foreign climes.

Pioneers in the field of private trolleybus preservation were members of the Reading Transport Society which acquired Reading 113, a 1939 Park Royal-bodied AEC 661T, from the Corporation in 1961. More trolleybuses from Reading and other fleets were soon added to its collection, for which a permanent home was sought.

Part of the former aerodrome at Sandtoft, near Doncaster, was acquired in 1969 and a museum developed jointly with the Doncaster Omnibus & Light Railway Society, West Riding Transport Society and Notts & Derby Transport Society. The last pair have since ceased to exist and the Bradford Trolleybus Association has more recently contributed to the museum's running and upkeep.

The first trolleybus ran at Sandtoft in 1972, just a few months after Bradford's last, since when the Trolleybus Museum at Sandtoft has developed such that it now houses the largest number of preserved trolleybuses kept at a single location, each owned by contributing societies, groups or individuals. The museum also has the most complex overhead wiring, allowing a wide range of manoeuvres to be undertaken on any one demonstration run. The

Reading Transport Society was renamed the British Trolleybus Society in 1971 as its membership spread nationwide and has its own fleet of 12 trolleybuses including London Transport 1812, repatriated from Spain and extensively restored to original condition.

The Sandtoft site itself has been developed over the past four decades to include a 1950s/60s streetscape complete with period shop displays, a prefab bungalow and other memorabilia from the era. It has also earned accreditation from the Museums, Libraries and Archives Council, which sets nationally-agreed standards for museums, and is a Quality Assured Visitor Attraction under a programme run by VisitEngland.

From Sandtoft we move southwards along the east coast to a second preserved trolleybus mainstay, the East Anglia Transport Museum at Carlton Colville.

The Museum itself dates from 1966 when a two-acre meadow was set aside by Mr A V Bird for the East Anglia Transport Society to develop a transport museum. The first trolleybus (London Transport 1521, a 1940 Metro-Cammell chassisless) arrived later the same year and the London Trolleybus Preservation Society erected its first depot shed at the museum two years later.

London 1521 moved under its own power in

Crossing the Black Country Living Museum's tram line in June 2006 is resident ex-Walsall Corporation 862 (TDH 912), a 1955 Willowbrook-bodied Sunbeam F4A.

Bradford Corporation 735 (DKY 735), a 1945 Karrier W, was rebodied by East Lancs in 1959 with this forward entrance body as part of the Bradford fleet's modernisation. This saw a number of second-hand acquisitions and older vehicles rebodied. This bus has received an 8ft wide body on a 7ft 6ins wide chassis – the front axle has been modified to suit but the rear axle retains its narrower track. Forward-entrance double-deck trolleybuses were uncommon.

1971 although regular trolleybus operation at Carlton Colville had to wait another decade until the museum's internal road network was sufficiently developed. A turning circle at Chapel Road was added in 1995 and, from 2008, a circular trolleybus service was run with the opening of Herting Street.

The museum has long been regarded as the home of the preserved London trolleybus with three examples owned by the London Trolleybus Preservation Society alongside its provincial and overseas trolleybuses. Visitors can enjoy rides on trolleybuses dating from 1926 to 1989 as the museum hosts the oldest and newest operational preserved trolleybuses in this country – a 1926 ex-Copenhagen Garrett and a 1989 ex-Athens ZiU 682G1.

England's first regional open-air museum was established at Beamish, County Durham, in 1970 by a consortium of Cleveland, Durham, Northumberland and Tyne & Wear County Councils. The public were

Former Maidstone Corporation 56 (GKP 511), a 1944 Sunbeam W with 1960 Roe bodywork, at the Black Country Living Museum in 2006. It was one of a number of British trolleybuses built during the war or in the immediate post-war period to be rebodied at a later date owing to the use of inferior bodywork materials when constructed. The local period adverts are a nice finishing touch.

admitted from 1972 since when its attractions have included a trio of trolleybuses, two of which remain resident. These are Newcastle 501, a 1948 Northern Coachbuilders-bodied Sunbeam S7, and Keighley 12, a 1924 Brush-bodied Straker-Clough trackless which was acquired in 1988 after use as a Grassington holiday home and awaits restoration. The third, ex-Teesside 5, a 1950 Sunbeam F4 rebodied by Roe in 1965 with the last trolleybus body to be built in the UK, has now resided for some years at Kirkleatham Old Hall in a purpose-built shed.

The museum's Edwardian period setting has limited use of its trolleybus overhead leading to Newcastle 501 being loaned to Sandtoft and Carlton Colville for varying periods. However, plans have been announced for the construction of a 1950s themed area which is anticipated to include trolleybus operation through a shopping area complete with cinema and theatre.

Other regional open-air museums followed, including the Black Country Living Museum at Dudley in 1978. The museum's road network houses this country's longest trolleybus route at just under a mile, and this is operated on Sundays and Bank Holidays by the Black Country Living Museum Transport Group's trolleybuses.

Theft of a length of overhead by scrap metal thieves in January 2011 forced a halt until the circuit was re-erected in March 2012. An emphasis on Black Country trolleybus operators has seen some vehicles

Portsmouth Corporation 313 (ERV 938), a 1951 Burlingham-bodied BUT 9611T, made its post-restoration debut at Carlton Colville in 2007. It is seen that year at the Twilight Trolleybus event in September.

depart for pastures new leaving four trolleybuses at the museum. These are Wolverhampton 78, a 1931 all-Guy BTX which awaits rebuilding after recovery from Ireland; Wolverhampton 433, a 1946 Sunbeam W with 1959 Roe body; Walsall 862, a 1955 Willowbrook-bodied Sunbeam F4A and Bradford 735, a 1946 Karrier W with 1959 East Lancs body which it is intended will masquerade as a Walsall trolleybus.

Elsewhere, other operational trolleybuses are owned by the National Trolleybus Association which was formed in 1963 to acquire and preserve trolleybuses, with some 15 owned by 1972. A number were later passed to other groups and a core collection of five vehicles retained. Two of these are in full working order, Bournemouth 202, a 1935 Park Royal-bodied Sunbeam converted to open-top in 1958 and based at Carlton Colville, and Huddersfield 541, a 1947 Park Royal-bodied Karrier MS2 which is at Sandtoft. The other three are Belfast 168, a 1948 Harness-bodied Guy BTX; Hastings 45, a 1928 Ransomes Sims & Jefferies-bodied Guy BTX, and Wolverhampton 654, a 1949 Park Royal-bodied Guy BT and these are undergoing or awaiting restoration at private sites.

Another trolleybus stronghold is the Ipswich Transport Museum with seven ex-Ipswich Corporation trolleybuses in its collection. These are 2, a 1923 Short-bodied Railless; 9, a 1926 all-Ransomes Sims & Jefferies D; 16, a 1926 Ransomes Sims & Jefferies D chassis; 26, a 1926 Strachan &

Bournemouth Corporation received 39 of these distinctive dual-doorway Weymann-bodied Sunbeam MF2Bs in 1958-59 and 1962, complete with exit doors ahead of the front axle. 286 (YLJ 286) was built in 1959 and operated in its home town for ten years before sale to Wombwell Diesels (dealers) and swift resale to the London Trolleybus Preservation Society. It has resided at Carlton Colville since 1972 and is seen here in September 2011.

The Trolleybus Museum at Sandtoft held a London event over the 2012 August Bank Holiday weekend to mark the completed restoration of former London Transport 1348 (EXV 348), a 1939 all-Leyland LPTB70 placed on long-term loan to the Museum by the Irish Transport Museum Society. It is seen on the right in the company of Sandtoft resident 1812 (HYM 812), a 1948 Metro-Cammell-bodied BUT 9641T, and the Carlton Colville-based London Trolleybus Preservation Society's 260 (CUL 260), a 1936 Metro-Cammell-bodied AEC 663T.

Former Newcastle Corporation 501 (LTN 501), a 1948 Northern Coachbuilders-bodied Sunbeam S7 forms part of the North of England Open Air Museum's collection at Beamish but post-dates its period setting. It has recently been loaned to Sandtoft and the East Anglia Transport Museum where it seen in 2011.

Brown-bodied Garrett O Type; 46, a 1933 all-Ransomes Sims & Jefferies D; 105, a 1948 Park Royal-bodied Karrier W and 126, a 1950 Park Royal-bodied Sunbeam F4.

We now get to the ones, twos and threes – museums such as the National Museum of Science & Industry which has Ipswich 44, a 1930 all-Ransomes Sims & Jefferies D, and Brighton Hove & District 6340, a 1939 Weymann-bodied AEC 661T, in its large object store at Wroughton, near Swindon. Glasgow TBS13, a 1958 Burlingham-bodied BUT RETB/1, is at the city's Riverside Museum premises while the Ulster Folk & Transport Museum hosts Belfast 112, a 1948 Harkness-bodied Guy BTX.

Other museums with trolleybuses on static display include the Manchester Museum of Transport where there are Manchester 1250, a 1951 Crossley Dominion, and Ashton-under-Lyne 80, a 1950 Crossley Empire, the Keighley Bus Museum which is home to Keighley trackless 5, a 1924 Brush-bodied Straker Clough, and Bradford 844, a 1948 Sunbeam F4 with 1963 East Lancs body which was the UK's last service trolleybus, and the Transport Museum at Wythall where there is Wolverhampton 616, a 1949

KEY TROLLEYBUS COLLECTIONS

Black Country Living Museum
www.bclm.co.uk

East Anglia Transport Museum
www.eatm.org.uk

Ipswich Transport Museum
www.ipswichtransportmuseum.co.uk

London Transport Museum
www.ltmuseum.co.uk

Trolleybus Museum at Sandtoft
www.sandtoft.org.uk

Park Royal-bodied Sunbeam F4.

The Bournemouth Heritage Transport Association's collection of ex-Bournemouth, Bradford and Notts & Derby trolleybuses may be seen at their new home at the West of England Transport Collection, Winkleigh. A unique trolleybus may also be spotted in and around its home town of Hastings. Hastings Tramways 3, perhaps better known as 'Happy Harold', a 1928 Dodson open-top and open-staircase-bodied Guy BTX, was restored by Hastings Tramways in 1952 and fitted with a Commer TS3 diesel engine in 1960 to enable its continued use by Hastings Council after trolleybus operation ceased the previous year.

And let us not forget those trolleybuses out of the public eye, mostly in private secure storage but with one or two perhaps facing a less than certain future. Some, like Portsmouth 1, a 1934 English Electric-bodied AEC 661T, have led a nomadic existence in preservation, sometimes in the public eye and at other times hidden away. It is currently kept securely under cover with the City of Portsmouth Preserved Transport Depot collection.

More variety is made available as vehicles are made operational, often after lengthy and comprehensive restorations, or are imported or repatriated.

Sandtoft was in 2012 gifted the former Wellington 82, a 1964 Metro-Cammell-bodied BUT RETB/1, by the Omnibus Society of New Zealand. It is to be sent to Thamesdown Transport for bodywork restoration, as have the British Trolleybus Society's Manchester 1344, Walsall 872 and Huddersfield 631. This is nothing new as other trolleybuses have been subject to past commercial work at their owners' expense for a variety of reasons such as timing, practicality or a lack of expertise in a particular field.

Interest in trolleybus preservation has no doubt been boosted by a number of special events which in recent years have reunited, among others, surviving Bradford, Maidstone, Reading, Newcastle and London trolleybuses. The equally popular Gatherings, Twilight Trolleybuses, and suchlike remain as annual fixtures thanks to the armies of volunteers in public view and behind the scenes who make them happen: Thank you, ladies and gentlemen!

Every trolleybus undertaking had at least one tower wagon. Portsmouth Corporation owned two, a pair of 1933 Leyland Titan TD2s that were converted at its Eastney depot workshops into the form shown in 1955. The first, TW1 (RV 3411), is seen at Cosham Compound in 1996. TW1 is owned by Portsmouth City Museums and Records Service and currently resides in full working order with the City of Portsmouth Preserved Transport Depot collection.

East Midland
deregulated

JOHN YOUNG illustrates the East Midland fleet in the 1980s and 1990s.

The early days of deregulation in the late 1980s saw significant changes at East Midland Motor Services. There was a management buy-out of the business from NBC in February 1988, a new green and cream livery, and significant expansion. The traditional operations from bases at Chesterfield, Clowne, Mansfield, Retford, Shirebrook and Worksop were joined by new tendered services in Essex for London Transport, which ran under the Frontrunner name. Operations in the Glossop and High Peak area were acquired from Trent, and there was subsequent brief expansion in to Stockport, Manchester and Salford, also operated as Frontrunner. The company was bought by Stagecoach in April 1989, which quickly sold the southern operations to Ensign Bus, while the High Peak operations passed to Bee Line, part of the Drawlane Group.

A non-standard type purchased by East Midland in the NBC era was a batch of unusual boxy Alexander P-type Leyland Tigers, which were delivered in 1985. They seated 52 and proved to be reliable workhorses. One climbs past Mellor Church in April 1989 on a journey from Stockport to Glossop via New Mills and Hayfield.

Most of the buses in the East Midland fleet in the late 1980s were standard NBC models such as this 1984 Gardner-engined Leyland Olympian with 77-seat ECW body, seen arriving at Newark Bus Station in June 1989. It carries Mansfield District fleetnames.

An earlier generation of standard NBC double-decker loads in Sheffield Interchange in May 1989. It is a 1977 Bristol VRT with ECW body.

NBC also bought small numbers of Alexander TE-type express coach bodies on Leyland Tigers, as illustrated by this 1983 coach leaving Peak Dale in October 1989 on service X67 from Manchester to Mansfield. At one time this route ran all the way from Lincoln to Liverpool.

A 1978 Bristol LH6L in Matlock in May 1989 is operating local service 160 to Hackney, a route previously run by Trent. It has a 43-seat ECW body. The logos on either side of the destination proclaim: "East Midland Frontrunner, your reliable local bus."

Small buses in the post-deregulation East Midland fleet included MCW Metroriders bought both new and second-hand. This bus in Chesterfield in 1989 with Roadrunner branding had been new in 1987 and came from Avon Buses of Moreton. It seated 25.

The highbridge version of the Bristol VRT/ECW combination was relatively uncommon and perhaps looked a bit top heavy. This 1979 bus was still in NBC leaf green when photographed passing through Dinnington in January 1991 on the service to Rotherham.

Six Alexander-bodied Atlanteans joined the fleet from Grampian Regional Transport for use on tendered operations from Tintwistle outstation. This bus is in Hazel Grove, Stockport, operating a Greater Manchester PTE tendered service in April 1989. It was new in 1976 and it carries Frontrunner North West fleetnames.

Three dual-purpose Leyland National 2s were purchased in 1983. In 1987 this one was running in Essex as part of the short-lived Frontrunner South East operations. It is seen in Ongar.

Stagecoach added Chesterfield Transport to its portfolio in 1995. This brought Leyland Lynxes in to the East Midland fleet. One traverses the typically industrial surroundings of Brightside Lane between Meadowhall and Sheffield in September 1999. In contrast, the onward journey to Tideswell and Buxton will become more scenic.

In 1989 Stagecoach bought three tri-axle Leyland Olympians, the first three-axle diesel double-deck buses (as distinct from coaches) built for service in Britain for some 50 years. This one with Megadekka markings seated 110 and started its life in Glasgow but was soon transferred to East Midland. Here it arrives at the 1990 Showbus rally in the grounds of Woburn Abbey.

The acquisition of Chesterfield Transport added more National 2s to the fleet, including this bus seen in the plague village of Eyam in 1997 on a journey from Buxton to Chesterfield. The 1665 plague wiped out three quarters of the population of the village. The National was new in 1984 and had a Gardner engine.

In later years a batch of Dennis Darts new to Docklands Transit became regular performers on some of the Peak District routes, One heads out of Litton in January 2000 bound for Sheffield and Meadowhall. It had a 40-seat Plaxton Pointer body and was new in 1996.

FROM Ikarus to hybrid

The Ikarus 280 was the mainstay of the Leipzig city fleet at reunification. One of the few in fleet livery still retained its DDR registration when seen working northern cross suburban route N in July 1991.

DAVID COLE looks at how city buses in Leipzig have changed since German re-unification.

All photographs by the author.

The scenes from the evening of 9 November 1989 remain vividly in many peoples' memories. After 28 years as the symbol of the Cold War, the Berlin Wall was formally breached. Germans from East and West rejoiced and within a year the country was reunified ending 40 years of diverging development. When applied to East Germany, 'development' may be a slightly generous description, especially when considering aspects of road transport.

As part of what was commonly called Comecon, the Eastern Bloc equivalent of the common market, series production of full-sized passenger vehicles in the DDR – the German Democratic Republic - had all but ceased in 1959. Core DDR production had

been conservative to the end, the H6B was a solid single-deck workhorse with a vertical front engine adaptable to coach and bus use whilst, despite the smooth lines of the exterior, the snout nosed DO54/6 double-deckers offered passenger accommodation little changed from the Berlin double-deckers of the early 1930s. Under Comecon, the lead role for full-sized passenger vehicle production had been given to Hungary with the result that Ikarus became the world's largest bus manufacturer for many years. Post 1959, DDR production was on a small scale by the Fleischer company in Gera who continued to produce a limited number of luxury coaches.

By the time of the fall of the Berlin Wall, Ikarus buses with high floors and engines at the rear (solo models) or underfloor (articulated models) had come to dominate the bus scene in East Germany. Their dominance was, however, not total and operators had, amongst others, received small numbers of Polish Jelcz, Czech Skoda and thirsty

A fleet of 15 step-entrance MAN SL202s arrived in the summer of 1991 carrying the L-NV registration series which has been applied to all subsequent LVB city buses. A brand new bus is seen on former trolleybus route A at the Adler crossroads in south-west Leipzig, a major tram and bus interchange point.

petrol-engined Russian ZiL models, some of which had short lives. In most major cities, the tram was still the main form of mass transport although the centre of East Berlin, in line with many capital cities worldwide, became the domain of the bus and, to a lesser extent, the underground railway. Many of the Ikarus buses delivered to the DDR would operate initially in Berlin, being cascaded to provincial operators before the first overhaul was due, thus avoiding the need for major workshop capacity in the capital.

By comparison, on the western side of the Wall in 1989, operators still had the choice of vehicles made in Germany from Mercedes-Benz, MAN, Setra and Neoplan (the last two then independent) plus a number of specialists such as Vetter along with imports from surrounding EU countries. The low-floor revolution was underway and consideration was being given to alternative means of propulsion.

My introduction to provincial East German

transport came with a posting to Leipzig, the second largest city with a population of over half a million, shortly after reunification. Evenings and weekends gave the initial opportunity to explore the city and get to know its transport network. Subsequently, public transport was to prove a more practical way of getting around the increasingly congested city on business as well. My posting lasted to the end of 1991 but thanks to friends made at the time, I have seen the city's transport operations develop on almost annual visits, following the bus network within the city boundaries from the Ikarus domination of 1991 to the varied hybrid fleet 20 years later.

In summer 1991, the bus played a significantly subservient role within the city to Leipzig's tramway network, both being operated by a reconstituted but still state-owned LVB AG (Leipzig Verkehrsbetriebe AG). It would be January 1993 before the company was reformed as LVB GmbH, a limited company

Seen at the main railway station in June 1996 on service 52 (Sundays-only tram replacement predecessor of the 72) is one of the 45 MAN NL202 buses delivered in the first half of the 1990s.

The standard LVB articulated bus during the 1990s was the Mercedes-Benz O405GN. This one is seen in August 2000 waiting to turn into the main railway station interchange to pick up a 73 working to Baalsdorf.

When first delivered in 1998, the Volvo B10Ls appeared on the high-profile 72/3 services passing the main railway station. This bus is seen on a damp day in October that year.

The Mercedes-Benz O407s which started life with Kraftverkehr Leipzig gained a silver livery when transferred with the airport service to LVB in 1997. One arrives at the main railway station in September that year.

owned 83% by the city of Leipzig and 17% by Landkreis Leipzig, the authority responsible for the city's rural hinterland.

The only buses regularly to be found in the city centre at that time were on a small number of interurban services and the airport express, all provided by regional operators based outside of the city. LVB buses, however, provided most of the cross suburban links and feeder services to the extremities of the tram network.

Route development

In 1991, two significant routes maintained a link with the city's trolleybus system which had been finally abandoned in 1975. These were A, the main southern cross-suburban link, and B, linking to the adjacent town of Markranstaedt. Much of the third

trolleybus route, the C to Zwenkau, had disappeared through the encroachment of open-cast brown coal mines and the replacement was no longer an LVB service, being provided instead by the Zwenkau-based RVL (Regional Verkehr Leipzig). All other bus services were also lettered, often with some geographical relevance such as H for the shuttle to Holzhausen. In addition to A and B, the other most significant routes were the N and W, cross-suburban links in the north and west of the city and the M/Z from the periphery of the city centre to villages on the eastern outskirts.

By 1997, with a regional transport body in prospect, the almost 70-year-old route letter system was in need of replacement. From 5 October 1997, route numbers were given to the bus network, starting at 60 to avoid duplication of tram route

LEFT: **The Mercedes-Benz Citos delivered in 1999 provided the first regular bus service within the city ring, route 89 also replacing tram 24. In August 2000, one negotiates narrow city centre streets passing the Riquet chocolate shop with its distinctive elephant head entrance.**

RIGHT: **The striking Mercedes-Benz Citaro-based Silberpfeil vehicles delivered in 1999 were to a Hannover design and many operated in that city during Expo 2000. This bus is seen in Hannover in September 2000.**

numbers. The 10 multiples 60, 80, 90 were given to the main cross-suburban routes A, W and N. The 70 would come along later, the four routes then overlapping to give an almost complete outer ring.

The regional transport body, MDV (Mitteldeutscher Verkehrsverbund) was formed in March 1998 although common tariffs were not implemented until August 2001. Further structural change was planned for 1999, when the Leipzig city boundaries were to be redrawn. This had the potential to bring a significant volume of the work undertaken by regional operator RVL within the city boundary. Negotiations on a merger had started in 1998 and LVB acquired 95% of RVL from 1 January 1999. The current Leobus name was adopted in 2005 when city and regional operations were combined.

No time was lost in introducing a common LVB/

RVL network with new interchanges to minimise parallel running. RVL routes took numbers from 100 upwards, 100 being allocated to a new express service from the tramway interchange at Connewitz to Zwenkau, RVL's base. In a reversal of previous changes, the 100 was extended to Leipzig Hauptbahnhof (the main railway station) in July 2002. A second express route, the 131, also serving Hauptbahnhof, was introduced in August 2004 westwards to Merseburg, the local service having previously terminated at Angerbrucke tram depot.

Buses took on a new role in August 1998 with the introduction of the 'Night Liner' routes N1-N9 providing all-night services to all parts of the city. Buses would also provide some evening and weekend replacements for tram services, most notably route 70 which covered the 22 around the

The first Solaris Urbino 12s arrived in 2005 with Euro 3 engines. This bus, with a distinctive livery for Leipzig Zoo, is seen in September 2006 on route 89 past the city's old town hall.

eastern suburbs from August 1999.

The late 1990s brought a series of new routes as the tram network was aligned to changes in major passenger flows. Tram route 2 to Anger-Crottendorf, an area of significant depopulation, succumbed to bus routes M/Z shortly before they became the 72/3 in 1997. These routes from the villages of Baalsdorf and Engelsdorf already paralleled the tram route at its eastern end and were diverted from their previous peripheral terminus to follow the tram route past the Hauptbahnhof interchange to reach Plagwitz and (off peak, a year later) the main bus depot at Lindenau. In 2003, trams were reintroduced to Plagwitz and the 72/3 cut back to the Hauptbahnhof.

The 24 through the musicians quarter in the south of the city was the next tram casualty in October 1999, the replacement bus route, midibus-operated 89, covered the short length of abandoned tram track with new routing at either end. Particularly significant was the routing through the central shopping area, bringing public transport back within the city's tramway inner ring for the first

time since 1951. Transponder-operated bus gates allowed access to the pedestrianised area around the historic market place. In July 2002, the routing at the southern end was revised to improve connections, whilst the midibuses later gave way to full-size vehicles.

LVB introduced possibly the most significant revision ever of its tram network from 27 May 2001 which also resulted in a number of additional bus facilities. The 70 became an all day bus operation allowing some of the tracks used by tram route 22 to be abandoned. A further tangential route, the 79, appeared in the north-east of the city and the first minibus feeder service, replacing a lightly-used tramway branch, was introduced in the western suburb of Leutsch.

The new network proved successful and the bus network, apart from a number of extensions to serve new developments such as the new BMW factory and the DHL freight hub, was to change little over the next nine years. Some evening facilities were replaced by pre-bookable taxi operations under the designation Anlita (Anruf Linien Taxi) or AST (Anruf

LVB's first hybrid, a Solaris Urbino 18 with a US concept driveline initially operated on route 60, seen here opposite the Bayrische Bahnhof in September 2009; subsequently it was more likely to be found on the 72/3. The vehicle's 2007 registration number represents its year of delivery.

Later Solaris U12 deliveries had EEV engines and a roof-mounted drivers' air-conditioning unit. A new U12 takes up service on the 73E at the main railway station in September 2009.

The first series delivery of hybrid vehicles arrived in 2011, entering service on routes 72/3 before moving to the 60 as new Solaris U18s arrived. Outside the railway station is a Hess SwissHybrid in September 2011.

Sammel Taxi).

Faced with funding challenges, RVL services outside of the city boundary were significantly reviewed in December 2009 at the same time as changes were made to local rail services. Funding issues also led to the temporary withdrawal in April 2011 of the suburban rail service to Gruenau, the massive DDR-era housing scheme in the west of the city. An extension of bus route 80 provided most of the links not covered by existing services whilst the midibus service within Gruenau itself, introduced a month earlier under the Gruenolino title, was also strengthened. The rail service is expected to resume when Leipzig's new city centre underground railway link is opened in December 2013.

The first major revision to the city bus network in nearly ten years took place in October 2010 under the title 'Mehr Bus' (More Bus). This comprised extensions and frequency improvements on many existing services, some rerouting and the elevation of the 74 to become a further significant cross suburban route in the south of the city.

The bus fleet

In 1991, the LVB fleet comprised some 150 vehicles, all of Ikarus manufacture except for ten MAN SL200 vehicles from the West German Vestische Strassenbahn company which had been donated to the city early in 1990. These retained their orange and cream livery, other buses carried a variety of colour schemes including the blue and cream of the trams, all over adverts and typical DDR mustard finish.

Six different Ikarus models were represented, two-axle 255/256/260 and 263 models plus the articulated 280 in three door city (S) and two door interurban (L) versions. With around 80 examples including several former Berlin vehicles and eight delivered as late as 1990, the manual gearbox 280S fleet worked most of the key routes including the frequent and heavily-loaded A. The 260 model formed the second largest group with over 50 of a once much larger fleet remaining in service.

Further new vehicles delivered in 1990 were in total contrast to the last Ikarus deliveries, four Neoplan Cityliner coaches to help satisfy the demand for travel pent up during 28 years of isolation from the west. Three of them were sold in 1994, the fourth lasting until 2001, when it was replaced by a new Mercedes-Benz Tourismo O350, and became the Leipzig Lions American Football Team coach.

The first deliveries of standard West German

Solaris deliveries in 2009 included five Alpino midibuses of which this bus was the 50th Solaris vehicle delivered to LVB, as marked by lettering on the windscreen. It carries route branding for the Gruenolino service but is working route 87 in Leipzig's northern suburbs in June 2012.

buses arrived in summer 1991, the 15 MAN SL202 solobuses were to be the fleet's only new non-low-floor SLII standard buses. Finished in a new livery featuring the city colours of yellow and blue, they entered service initially on route A where the shine of their paintwork made them stand out from most other vehicles on the road at the time. From 1992 onwards, low-floor vehicles were specified in significant quantities, 45 MAN NL202 solobuses arrived over the next three years whilst the initial requirement for articulated buses was met with the delivery of 24 Mercedes-Benz O405GN over a six-year period.

The move towards standardisation was interrupted in 1996 when a Europe-wide tendering process led to the delivery of four Volvo B10Ls with bodywork constructed at the Steyr plant in Austria. They were to prove unpopular and were cascaded out of the main LVB fleet in 2003. There was a

return to MAN in 1997 for three of the updated NL223 model, whilst four Mercedes-Benz O407s were transferred from RVL, in advance of the latter's acquisition, together with the contract for the airport service.

Leipzig had developed strong political links with Hannover in advance of reunification and the effects of this permeated many of the city's activities including transport. Hannover planned a major exhibition, Expo, to run throughout 2000 celebrating the millennium which would require significant numbers of additional vehicles and drivers. Leipzig played a significant role with the provision of 25 vehicles and drivers for route 124 Expo to Misburg. The vehicles came from a batch of 30 Mercedes-Benz Citaro articulated buses matching the then current Hannover styling from British designer James Irvine. They featured extra doorways for rapid loading, and limited seating with relatively few forward-facing

seats. Externally they were finished in a new silver-based livery in Hannover style and were christened 'Silberpfeil' (silver arrow). They may have looked different, but they proved not to be immune to the engine compartment fires experienced by some other Citaro operators.

The return of the Silberpfeil from Hannover enabled the final Ikarus vehicles to be taken out of service. The last three, withdrawn in March 2001, had survived long enough to gain the blue and yellow livery and were cascaded, like many other LVB vehicles, to the RVL subsidiary. The solo Ikarus buses had already bowed out of LVB service in August 1999, at the same time as the Vestische MAN SL200s. One of the latter was converted to a mobile information unit.

In parallel with the Silberpfeil delivery, LVB received five Mercedes-Benz Cito midibuses with diesel-electric drive for use mainly on the new 89 service. In 2001 they were fitted with CRT filters to further reduce their environmental impact within the city centre before being moved out to some of the shorter suburban services where they joined two Mercedes-Benz Sprinters acquired in 2003.

With all of the DDR-era fleet replaced in less than ten years, further new full-size vehicles did not join the fleet until 2005 when the first batch of Polish-built Solaris Urbino 12s arrived. The first seven were the only Euro 3 examples of this model, further deliveries from 2006 to 2010 being to EEV standard with DAF Euro 5 engines. These brought the Solaris U12 fleet up to 60 vehicles, facilitating replacement of all the MAN solo buses. Five additional Solaris delivered in 2009 introduced the Cummins-engined Alpino 8.6m midibus model for the type of role previously undertaken by the Cito fleet. All Solaris deliveries have featured the silver, blue and yellow

ABOVE: **The Leobus fleetname is carried on regional services vehicles operated from Zwenkau depot, including this 15m Mercedes-Benz Citaro seen passing the Leipzig Opera House in September 2011.**

RIGHT: **The 'Paris Bus' phase of Leipzig city tour operations is represented by a green-liveried example in September 2009. Others carried red or yellow liveries.**

colour scheme introduced with the Silberpfeil although a number have been wrapped in all over advertising.

At the 2006 LVB autumn festival (Herbstauftakt) held in the Lindenau bus depot, the company presented a series of demonstration vehicles from MAN, Mercedes-Benz, Volvo and Solaris for customer feedback. Subsequent acquisitions continued to be from Solaris. Buses were again at the fore for the final Herbstauftakt held in 2008 when the undertaking was considering a return to trolleybus operation. Neoplan displayed an export trolleybus and Hess a double-articulated LighTram.

LVB had already received its first hybrid in September 2007, the vehicle subsequently appearing on the Solaris stand at the 2007 Busworld Kortrijk show. This first-generation Urbino U18 hybrid articulated vehicle featured a US-proven combination of side-mounted Cummins ISLe4 8.9-litre diesel engine with GM Allison parallel hybrid drive to the second axle. Externally it was distinguished by a large roof pod to house batteries and control equipment together with green motifs on the standard LVB livery. European industry was quick to develop a second generation of hybrid design more suited to local requirements and this was chosen by LVB over the trolleybus project as the way forward in improving environmental performance. The Saxhybrid and RegioHybrid projects with other transport operators in the state of Saxony enabled LVB to secure government and state funding for delivery of hybrids in 2011.

Eighteen hybrids from three manufacturers entered service in 2011, the largest contingent being ten Hess articulated vehicles with Iveco 5.8-litre diesel engines, Vossloh Kiepe series hybrid drive to two axles and supercap energy storage. These entered service mainly on the 72/3 group of routes, giving them a high profile at the Hauptbahnhof main interchange. They were joined on these routes by three Mercedes-Benz Citaro G Blue-tec articulated series hybrids where they replaced 15-year-old Mercedes-Benz O405GNs. Last to arrive were the five Polish-built MAN Lions City solo hybrids for city service 89. The new hybrids carry a revised livery of light blue and grey with small areas of traditional blue and yellow, overlain by a ribbon of green leaves.

Investment in new vehicles for the regional

Royal London Bus's fleet appropriately includes this Routemaster, former London Transport RM 641, seen outside the Opera House in September 2010.

The Bristol FLF played a significant role in the Royal London Bus fleet in September 2010, one with reduced height and the entrance relocated to the right-hand side is being passed by the latest in LVB trams opposite the main railway station. The Lodekka carries London Transport fleetnames and displays Royal Albert Hall as its destination. It was new to Hants & Dorset.

services has also stepped up in recent years with 21 full-size new vehicles delivered since 2008 including four 15m three-axle Mercedes-Benz Citaros for the 100 Express service. These maintain the variety in a fleet which also includes MAN, Neoplan and Setra products and has extensively tested a number of demonstrators including a Ukrainian MAZ and a Dutch VDL Citea. The Solaris Electrobus has also been demonstrated to officials in the nearby town of Markkleeberg.

Since reunification, the composition of the LVB fleet has therefore gone almost full circle. Starting with a fleet almost exclusively of imported Ikarus vehicles, a fully 'made in Germany' fleet had been established early in the new millennium only to be subsequently replaced by further imports from Poland and Switzerland. The order for 45 Solaris Urbino 18 articulated vehicles announced in 2012 with a three-year delivery programme commencing at the end of that year will complete the latest generation change.

Sightseeing buses

No review of bus operations within the city of Leipzig would be complete without a mention of the sightseeing services which have proliferated in recent years. LVB's own tours have traditionally been by tram and specially adapted Tatras now undertake this task. Bus-based operation has been much more varied from Dotto-type trains through to the present Pan-European offering of historic vehicles from a number of operators including Leipziger Oldtimer Fahrten, Saechsische Oldtimer Busflotte Leipzig and, appropriately having started with a Routemaster, Royal London Bus Leipziger Sightseeing.

The mix of vehicles has grown over the years and from time to time certain types appear to be in the ascendancy. For a period this was the Paris open-platform single-decker, a few years later and the Bristol FLF Lodekka, with lowered roof line and offside exit was to the fore. The Lodekkas were in various styles of red livery with some carrying London Transport fleetnames.

Berlin double-deckers of various eras are a current growth area, from the D2U of the 1960s to the recently-retired low-floor double-deckers of the 1990s. Swiss post buses and an early Setra S80 coach also feature whilst various 'cabrio' single-deckers are popular on summer sightseeing tours in good weather.

You can almost hear the bus saying "It was never like this in London" as this ECW-bodied Bristol LH, formerly operated by London Buses, eases its way carefully through the ancient town walls of Alnwick in August 1994. Owned by Northumbria Motor Services it was one of 95 built for London operation.

A tight
fit

It is not always an easy task driving a bus or coach through a miscellany of hazards. **TONY WILSON** pays photographic tribute to those drivers who have to negotiate a variety of arches, bridges and other obstacles.

A former Rossendale East Lancs-bodied Leyland Atlantean of Alpine Travel of Llandudno wends its way carefully through one of the walled arches at Conwy, North Wales, in September 2002 on a Guide Friday franchised tourist service. Operated every 30 minutes during the high season it toured around Conwy and Llandudno with a live guide.

LEFT: In the early 1950s London Transport took 76 AEC Regent IIIs with Weymann lowbridge bodies for routes where highbridge vehicles could not be used. There were 32 red buses for four Central Area routes with the remainder being in green for the Country Area. By August 1980 all had been withdrawn but a few were operated occasionally by preservationists on special running days. One passes beneath the 13ft 3in railway bridge just south of Staines.

Unlike the older walled arches, this structure was one of many created in the 19th century to carry railway lines over roads, rivers and other obstacles. A Wright-bodied Volvo B6 from the South Yorkshire First Mainline subsidiary passes beneath the former railway line at Parsley Hay in June 2002 on route 181, part of the Summer Sunday Peak Bus network. With the actual railway long since closed the trackbed had been converted as a walking and cycle facility known as the Tissington Trail.

In July 1994 a Leyland National from the Chesterfield Transport fleet negotiates its way through the narrow walled roads of Uppertown Bonsall in the Derbyshire Peak District above Matlock. The driver has just completed a difficult reversing turn at the end of the route, again surrounded by the solid structures of buildings and dry stone walls, before returning back down the narrow twisting lanes to Matlock Town via Cromford and Matlock Bath.

In the 1970s Western National operated most of the stage services in Cornwall, and these included the 508 that served the fishing village of Mousehole. The only route in and out of the village and onto the quayside was along a very narrow street. A short and narrow 1972 Marshall-bodied Bristol LHS6L leaves the village on the route back to Penzance.

Cornwall is still served by Western National, but the company is now part of FirstGroup. A Mercedes-Benz Vario with Plaxton Beaver 2 body squeezes between the buildings on either side of a narrow street in Mevagissey in April 2008. The bus had been part of a large fleet new in 1998 to Midland Red West.

Another tight squeeze is experienced daily on route 272 between Sheffield and Castleton deep in the Derbyshire Peak District. The service is run jointly by First South Yorkshire and Hulleys of Baslow. Double-deckers are generally used and all pass through the quaint village of Bradwell, as illustrated in June 2012 by a 12-year-old Hulleys Volvo B7TL with Alexander ALX400 body which was originally operated by the London Central subsidiary of the Go-Ahead Group.

In July 1971 a Bristol SUL4A in the Southern Vectis fleet makes its way to the top end of a winding cul-de-sac at Luccombe. At the end the driver has to complete a several-point turn before he returns his charge down the hill to Sandown and Shanklin. The bus has a 36-seat ECW body and an Albion engine and was new in 1963.

Another Hulleys bus, this time a Leyland Lynx, roars its way up from the valley below onto the top of Monsal Head in April 2003. Two weekday journeys each day left the basic route of the 173 between Bakewell and Castleton and operated via Monsal Dale and Cressbrook. In doing so they paralleled for a short distance the former railway line through this spectacular countryside. Previously this Lynx, new in 1990, had operated for West Midlands Travel; this was certainly quite different terrain for the bus.

Many narrow lanes were traversed by this Northern Counties Palatine II bodied Volvo Olympian, seen here leaving Mundesley for Trunch in September 2005, when operated by Sanders Coaches. The "City Centre" in the destination is Norwich. Originally operated by Harris Bus on contracted routes in London, the odd lower deck window arrangement shows where the second door had been removed.

Bristol VRTs of Stagecoach subsidiary Cumberland were often seen on the 108 route during the 1990s, running westwards out of Penrith through the striking scenery of Patterdale to a terminus at Glenridding. This is September 1998, and an ECW-bodied VRT negotiates the narrow bridge in the village of Pooley Bridge at the southern end of Ullswater.

BELOW The 1993 summer season route network on the Isle of Wight featured several open-topped double-deckers operated by Southern Vectis. A few Bristol Lodekkas were among the vehicles used, as shown here by one negotiating the narrow hairpin-twisted roadway on the National Trust property that leads up from Alum Bay to the Needles Battery.

ABOVE: **Arriva Cymru operated a fleet of Plaxton-bodied Mercedes-Benz Varios. A 1998 bus is seen soon after delivery, passing along a narrow lane near Penmon on the Isle of Anglesey, brushing the hedgerows as it does so.**
BELOW **One of two former Maidstone & District open-topped AEC Regals which were operated during the late 1990s and early 2000s by Guide Friday on a seasonal tourist service based on Bourton-on-the-Water in the Cotswolds. The Cotswold Tour took in the delightful and quaint villages of Upper and Lower Slaughter. This bus was new in 1946.**

Chasing
the Greyhound

Buses editor **ALAN MILLAR** looks at how express coach travel has changed since 1972, when the talk was of a British equivalent of the iconic Greyhound brand in America.

Some people would have you believe that Britain lacked any sort of countrywide network of express coach services before 1972, when the National Bus Company introduced the single corporate identity that a few years later was called National Express.

Those people, surely, are not readers of *Buses Yearbook*. But 1972 was a turning point. The beginning of an era that allowed NBC, its successors, collaborators and competitors to promote express coach travel as a place-to-place, coast-to-coast public transport service throughout England and Wales, and increasingly beyond. Before then, it was an extensive patchwork of regionally marketed services.

That turning point was one of the building blocks that ensures that express coaches today carry well in excess of 20 million passengers a year — 16 million on National Express, 4 million on the Scottish Citylink/ Stagecoach megabus joint venture alone — despite the recent upsurge in travel by train and the relentless growth in car ownership and use.

But it only was a turning point. Express coach travel grew rapidly in the 1920s, hitting a prewar peak in demand in 1932 when 19 million journeys were recorded, thanks to advances in vehicle design and a booming market for travel as people moved in pursuit of better housing and jobs, women began to spend less time tied to their family homes, and holidays with pay became a national entitlement.

Those also were the years when key parts of the infrastructure were built. Digbeth coach station in Birmingham opened (as a bus depot) in 1929 and Victoria Coach Station in London followed in 1932. Both have been modernised several times over in the intervening years but despite serious attempts to replace and relocate them, they are exactly where they were built — on the edges of two of England's largest city centres.

By the end of the 1930s, most express coach services were provided by railway-owned regional bus companies, each with its own local or regional

Smartly dressed passengers preparing to board a 30-seat Alexander-bodied Guy Arab LUF of Western SMT on the overnight Glasgow-London service. The coach was new in 1955 and had a toilet compartment in the offside rear. JIM THOMSON

identity and its own ideas of what made an ideal coach, although some broadened customer choice by pooling their operations into jointly marketed networks such as Associated Motorways, with its coordinated daily interchange in Cheltenham.

The 1930 Road Traffic Act also gave the railways a statutory right of objection to new road service licence applications, which helps explain why demand peaked as early as 1932 and almost certainly limited innovation and expansion then and for over 30 postwar years.

What started changing the potential for coach travel were motorways, beginning with the Preston bypass in 1958 and the Watford-Crick section of the M1 (and M10 and M45 branches) in November 1959. Sustained high-speed running would reduce journey times and improve comfort over what was possible on largely single carriageway roads with twists, turns, gradients and delays through town and city centres.

Midland Red rose to the occasion with fast new single-deck coaches between Birmingham and London, while Ribble's Standerwick subsidiary put 50-seat Leyland Atlantean double-deckers on Lancashire-London services, complete with table service and a brand name that worked at the time: Gay Hostess.

NBC is born

The route to the creation of National Express began in 1969 when almost all the territorial bus companies of England and Wales came together in National Bus Company ownership.

Initially, it was business as usual with local brands identifying coach and bus services, and Standerwick began replacing its Atlanteans with a new fleet of longer 60-seat Bristol VRL double-deckers. Most other subsidiaries replaced their older single-deck coaches with longer ones, but aside from taking advantage of the steady expansion of the motorway network, little else changed that was radical.

Towards the end of 1971, however, the Conservative government installed a businessman as NBC's new chairman. Freddie (later Sir Freddie) Wood came from adhesives manufacturer Croda and had a vision of a single identity for buses and coaches. Reality, local resistance and perhaps a degree of humility tempered his ideas for buses, but coaches were another matter.

Like others before and after, he fell for an American dream. Greyhound, the largest and most enduring of that continent's coast-to-coast coach services was and is a national icon. It figures in movies and captures an essence of American life as potent as Cadillac cars or Coca-Cola.

By the 1970s, rising car ownership and domestic air travel expansion were beginning to dent the icon and make Greyhound decreasingly relevant for many Americans, but to be fair to Freddie Wood, that is a lot more obvious from 40 years' distance than it would have been then.

NBC's inheritance of separately identified and separately marketed coach services the length and breadth of England and Wales could be brought together, along with coach holidays, into a single brand equivalent of Greyhound. It was National, with white coaches, a bold brand name in red and blue capitals, an NBC double-N logo intended to be as recognisable as British Rail's double arrow of 1965, and a small local fleetname (later made a trifle bigger) to try and mollify those who mourned the end of Standerwick, Royal Blue, Midland Red, United, East Kent, Southdown and other strong regional names and liveries.

Wood's intention was to match a Greyhound-like identity with an upgrade in vehicle design to offer uniformly higher standards of comfort on National routes. It took a lot longer, and several changes of ownership and direction, for that to happen.

Ironically, the smaller part of the state-owned British express coach business had already cracked that nut. The Scottish Bus Group operated mainly overnight year-round services linking Edinburgh and Glasgow with London, as well as some routes to other English destinations mainly in partnership with Ribble and a few other NBC subsidiaries.

The London routes were perceived as the jewels in the SBG crown, operated exclusively by Eastern Scottish and Western SMT with no NBC involvement. From the 1950s, they had specified toilets in these coaches at a time when few British vehicles had them, as well as big reclining seats with generous legroom. This was a high-cost, heavily-peaked operation, with two senior drivers per coach.

The opening of the M1 in 1959 prompted Midland Red to develop its high-speed C5 coach, reputed to be capable of 85mph, for the Birmingham-London service. This 54-year-old preserved example was operating more sedately at the Wythall Transport Museum in 2013. ALAN MILLAR

An Alexander M-type Bristol REMH of Western SMT loading for a Glasgow-London departure in 1971. The small trapezoid windows conveyed speed and conserved heat at night. ALAN MILLAR

The epitome of double-deck coach design at the start of the 1970s was the 60-seat 11m ECW-bodied Bristol VRL operated by Standerwick, which survived into the start of National white coach age. This preserved example has been restored to original condition. ALAN MILLAR

SBG had taken advantage of changes in legislation to increase capacity and reduce the number of duplicate coaches on busy nights, replacing 30-seaters with 11m 38-seaters, and in 1968 became one of the first British operators of 12m coaches, and certainly the first to buy them in any quantity.

These held 42 seats (increased later to 46), but SBG had looked to America and other overseas countries to design a coach that looked a lot more like a real Greyhound than anything run here before or since. The Alexander M-type body, built initially on Bristol REMH chassis, had ribbed side panels and small trapezoid-shaped windows straight out of Hollywood, the windows being double-glazed and of reduced dimension to keep passengers warmer at night.

Early in Freddie Wood's chairmanship, NBC bought a single M-type body, on a Leyland Leopard chassis, for evaluation. It also tried a Scania provided as part of Metro-Cammell Weymann's tie-up with the Swedish bus and truck builder, but it also remained unique.

Somehow that part of the British Greyhound dream was quietly forgotten and NBC stocked its fleets mainly with Leopards with all-seated (no toilets) bodies by Plaxton, Duple, ECW and Willowbrook that offered no obvious advance in passenger facilities over what they replaced. An overturning accident hastened the end of the Standerwick VRLs. Developing a new generation coach was hardly a priority for a network focused increasingly on meeting the travel needs of students and pensioners, but it perhaps should have been if business was to expand.

First wave of deregulation

The catalyst for bigger change was the Transport Act 1980, which in October that year removed the need for road service licensing on excursions, tours and express services with at least 30miles between stops.

It was meant to open the roads up to innovative and competing new services and NBC rose to the occasion by reviewing its scheduled service network and rebranding it as National Express. For a time it ran a television and print advertising campaign with a cartoon frog called Beeper and slogans like 'It's cheaper by Beeper'.

Beeper came and went in the blink of a bulging eye, but this — and some lengthy peak summer national rail strikes — proved to be the making of National Express, which expanded and saw off much of its new competition.

The highest profile casualty among the newcomers was British Coachways, a consortium of larger regional independent coach companies — including Wallace Arnold, Shearings, Grey-Green and Park's of Hamilton — which adopted a brand identity similar to British Airways' livery of the day and launched a 'me too' network of routes in competition with NBC and SBG.

One of its biggest weaknesses was lack of access to NBC and SBG's bus and coach stations, leaving it operating from kerbsides and substandard off-street facilities like the Kings Cross terminal in London, since lost to construction of the British Library. It struggled to establish itself and was in trouble well before it was disbanded in October 1982.

One of NBC's clever moves was to tie up with another of the newcomers, Trathens of Plymouth, which had innovated by introducing Neoplan Skyliner double-deckers, at-seat catering, video films and faster non-stop journeys between Plymouth, Exeter and London.

Rather than embarking on cutthroat competition, they joined forces to create National Express Rapide, a higher quality service using Trathens coaches not only on the M4/M5 corridor but also to other parts of the country, as well as its own vehicles.

Glasgow-based Cotters had launched something similar, branded Coachline, in competition with SBG on its London routes, charging a small premium for coaches with video, music and hostess service, but another contemporary Scottish venture would change the face of UK coach and bus operation more than anything else that happened in the 1980s.

This was the birth of the business that began as GT Coaches and soon renamed itself Stagecoach. It started with a Dundee-London overnight service that grew into something bigger.

Aside from an hourly Edinburgh-Glasgow route, SBG ran few interurban express services within Scotland. There were several long all-stops routes (eg Glasgow-Dundee, journey time almost 4hr) catering for shorter intermediate journeys and probably carrying more parcels than people from terminus to terminus. Most people made those journeys by train.

Stagecoach changed that. It extended the London service to Aberdeen and introduced an Edinburgh-Inverness route, enabling it to operate increasingly frequent daytime services between Glasgow and Aberdeen, and Inverness and Edinburgh. Perth, where Stagecoach was and is based, is a natural crossroads where these routes meet, enabling passengers to interchange.

SBG, which had rebranded its London routes with single a blue and white Scottish livery in 1976, was caught napping by Stagecoach and in 1983 launched Scottish Citylink, with a blue and yellow livery, for a growing network of services run partly in competition with Stagecoach and other newcomers.

NBC and SBG also began upgrading the standard of coaches operated on express services, both — but especially NBC — equipping fleets with the new tri-axle Metroliner double-decker from MCW. Some went on to the National Express network, while others were used on a growing number of regional routes on which NBC was allowing its local managers to develop distinct identities and brands within a more loosely applied corporate identity.

One was Oxford Citylink, along the M40 to Heathrow Airport and London, a route that to this day lacks a fast rail connection.

Closer to London, deregulation allowed Maidstone & District to develop Invictaway-branded coach services — some operated with long wheelbase Leyland Olympians — to and from the Medway Towns, tapping into a commuter market of lower income clerical staff who embraced a cheaper alternative to rail. The then family-owned The Kings Ferry was another operator to recognise the potential of that unique market.

Privatisation on the agenda

While many judged coach deregulation to have been a success, others — Conservative politicians especially — were disappointed that state-owned National Express was its chief immediate beneficiary. New legislation was passed to permit NBC to sell parts of its business, especially National Express and the coach touring business by then rebranded as National Holidays.

That was easier said than done. National Express was

British Coachways livery on a preserved coach from one of the participating fleets, Morris Bros of Swansea. It is a Plaxton Supreme-bodied Volvo B58. ALAN MILLAR

a marketing front for services delivered by the regional bus subsidiaries. It could be picked apart, but not overnight, and NBC seemed to stall for as long as it could to avoid effecting such a difficult privatisation.

However, the gloves were off by the time the Transport Act 1985 received the Royal Assent and NBC was obliged to prepare all its subsidiaries for sale. From then on, the relationship between National Express and the bus operating companies became a contractual one, with National Express specifying the routes and buying in the services from the operators. It also began to buy increasing numbers of services from independent operators.

Something similar happened in Scotland from 1985, when SBG restructured itself into smaller subsidiary companies, one of them Citylink. By then, SBG's London services were part of the Citylink portfolio, but privatisation was not yet on the agenda.

National Express was among the last NBC subsidiaries to be sold, to its management in March 1988. The British Coachways experience had ensured that Victoria Coach Station did not go to National Express, open access to all operators being assured by retaining it in public ownership and transferring it to London Regional Transport for a token £25.9million. The coach company had cost its management £10.1million to buy.

Within a year, it was trying once again to realise Sir Freddie Wood's Greyhound dream and create a higher standard of coach. This was the National Expressliner, a

A Neoplan Skyliner of Trathens operating a National Express Rapide service from a typically basic post-deregulation terminal near London Paddington station. ALAN MILLAR

bespoke version of the Plaxton Paramount 3500-bodied Volvo B10M, which came with a huge moulded double-N logo on its unglazed back panel and was available in two levels of finish, one for Rapide and a less elaborate interior for ordinary routes.

The controversial twist was that operators were obliged to lease their Expressliners from National Expressliners, a joint venture company involving National Express, Roadlease (Plaxton's leasing arm) and Volvo. This at a time when contract terms were being tightened up to raise standards and drive down the price operators were paid to run the routes.

But it was a first move to raise the standard of coach that passengers could expect to encounter when buying a ticket, potentially making the shape of the coach as recognisable as the livery, which was largely unchanged from 1980.

Citylink is sold

By then, SBG was being prepared for privatisation and Stagecoach was well on the way to transforming itself from a plucky little independent into a national and international transport group. August 1989 saw two parallel developments change the balance of power.

One saw Stagecoach sell its original express coach business to National Express, which initially rebranded it as Caledonian Express with a fleetname in corporate style. The other ended the joint operation of cross-border services by National Express and Scottish Citylink, plunging Citylink into competition with its erstwhile partner and giving operators the opportunity of going with the service provider offering the best terms.

Citylink was sold to its management the following year for a mere £265,000 and the competition persisted

The 100th Plaxton Expressliner to be sold, a 1990 Volvo B10M for National Welsh. PLAXTON

A 2001-registered Van Hool Alizée-bodied DAF SB3000 of Cambridge Coach Services in the final version of National Express Jetlink livery. ALAN MILLAR

until the inevitable happened and National Express — which had been through some ownership changes and floated on the stock market in December 1992 — acquired Citylink during 1993 for £5million, ended its cross-border business and turned it into a purely Scottish operation.

National Express Group was changing fast. It had acquired Travel West Midlands and was winning train-operating franchises. Among its rail gains (in 1997) was ScotRail, providing most services in Scotland. The Monopolies & Mergers Commission decreed that this was a step too far, giving the group too much of a hold on the public transport market, and ordered it to sell Citylink. Significantly given subsequent events, the MMC considered that coaches and trains competed for some of their traffic.

In 1998, Citylink was sold to London operator Metroline for £10.2million. Metroline became part of Singapore-based ComfortDelGro in 2000, and two years later Citylink expanded into the Republic of Ireland, which is largely another story for another day.

It may have lost its internal Scottish business, but National Express was expanding elsewhere. A restructure of the business in 1992 led to it acquiring Speedlink Airport Services from Drawlane Transport. Speedlink had grown out of NBC's London Country to operate the express link between Heathrow and Gatwick Airports.

Subsequently renamed Airlinks, Speedlink became the nucleus of a National Express business focused on ground transport opportunities at all London airports, running airside and landside buses within the airports and developing long-distance coach connections.

In one of its bigger acquisitions, in 1999 Airlinks bought Cambridge Coach Services from Blazefield Holdings. CCS, by then operating 22 coaches, was the last visible remnant of Premier Travel, the Cambridge independent whose bus and National Express coach operations had been bought by ex-NBC operator Cambus nine years earlier. It had developed routes linking Cambridge with Heathrow, Gatwick, Stansted and Luton.

Early in 2000, National Express acquired Airbus, London United's Heathrow-London service with a fleet of 19 Volvo Olympian coaches. It added Airbus to its coach travel brands, extending it to Stansted and — for a short time — Birmingham. By then, it also had Jetlink and Flightlink-branded coaches serving airports.

Another of National Express's railway developments impacted on the Stansted Airbus service. In July 2000, the group acquired Prism Rail, whose four franchises included West Anglia Great Northern, operating Stansted Express trains to London Liverpool Street.

That gave it a monopoly of ground connections to the airport, but rather than order a divestment the Office of Fair Trading exacted conditions from National Express, preventing it from reducing the coach service, raising fares unduly or blocking any competitors entering the market.

The arrival and huge expansion of low-cost airlines

The National Express livery applied from 2003 to 2007, displayed in Birmingham in 2006 on a then directly operated Irizar PB-bodied Scania K114. MARK DOGGETT

The most recent additions to Stagecoach's Oxford Tube service are 87-seat Van Hool Astromega double-deckers. RUSSELL YOUNG

A Plaxton Panther-bodied Volvo B12B of Oxford Bus Company branded for its X90 service to London. STEVE MASKELL

A Jonckheere Monaco-bodied MAN 24.350 double-decker, bought new for the Oxford Tube service in 1999, operating a Newcastle-London megabus. com service through Meadowhall, near Sheffield in 2007. DANIEL STAZICKER

helped ensure that there was business for everyone at Stansted, with Italian-owned Terravision — which only started operating its first service in Rome in 2002 — establishing low fare competition between the airport and central London.

Change of identity

National Express entered 2003 with a new corporate identity. After 30 years, the N-sign logo was dropped, replaced by large red and blue circles with an arrow. The fleetname was restyled in upper and lower case letters and the range of airport service brands and liveries disappeared, their place taken by National Express Airport. For all the changes, three key features were considered indispensable: the National Express name, red and blue lettering, and white coaches.

The timing of this proved fortunate, as new challengers were on the horizon, threatening the near monopoly the company still enjoyed in express coach travel.

First to catch the headlines was easyBus, one of several new businesses from Stelios (now Sir Stelios) Haji-Ionnou's easyGroup. The man who prefers to be known by his first name had founded the immensely successful easyJet budget airline in 1995 and was trying to shake up other markets with easy-branded businesses.

The word coming out during 2003 was that easyBus would run high frequency minibuses on intercity routes — London-Birmingham was the example mooted — with on-line fares starting at £1. It took until August 2004 for services to start, initially between Milton Keynes and Hendon Central towards a northern extremity of the London Underground Northern Line. Terminating there, rather than in central London, cut costs and avoided the worst congestion.

National Express hit back with low fares and easyBus gave up that route, opting instead to develop airport connections. A Luton Airport-Hendon route was extended later to Baker Street on the northern edge of central London. Today, it runs two other minibus services, Stansted-Baker Street and Gatwick-Earls Court/West Brompton, both feeding on to London Underground.

It still serves Luton, but until May 2013 it did this in a novel fashion that saw Arriva the Shires' Green Line-branded 757 service to Victoria operate a four-way ticket sales arrangement with three potential competitors. Coaches carried logos for easyBus, Terravision and National Express and — besides on-line sales opportunities — passengers arriving at Luton were met by sales desks from all four operators offering tickets at different prices for travel on the same service.

Once the brand name for London Transport's limited-stop coach services stretching out into surrounding towns, Green Line survives in the 21st century on a handful of routes, most operated by Arriva, which owns the name. Besides the 757, it runs commuter coaches from Luton, St Albans, Stevenage and Hemel Hempstead to London, an orbital bus route (724) between Harlow and Heathrow and First runs coaches and double-deckers between London and Windsor.

The Luton arrangement came to a sticky end in 2013 when the airport struck a seven-year deal with National Express that appeared to give it exclusive rights to provide a new service to Victoria. However, easyBus was able to restart its minibus service to Baker Street and Arriva kept the 757 running in competition with both of them, reaching agreement with one of the airport car parks to terminate its coaches there and transfer passengers on to a shuttle bus to/from the terminal buildings.

Megabus shakes up the market

If easyBus over-hyped and under-delivered, the opposite proved to be the case with the other challenger of 2003. This was megabus.com, one of several new ventures test-marketed by Stagecoach, which already had form with intercity coaches.

There had long been a view that as bus operations were consolidated into a new patchwork combination of former NBC and SBG companies, at least some of the big groups had the resources and scale — should they wish to — for a serious challenge to National Express. An added incentive was that most of the big groups — Stagecoach, First and Arriva among them — operated coaches on National Express contracts.

Stagecoach also had regional express coach services, with walk-on pay-the-driver fares more like a bus service. Its most intensive network operated across central Scotland, but since early 1996 it had run the high-frequency Oxford Tube along the M40 to London, started by Harry Blundred's Transit Holdings in competition with the Oxford Bus Company. With demand for both Oxford services continuing to grow and its rival differentiating itself by the quality of its

To meet growing demand for megabus services, Stagecoach worked with Plaxton to develop the 75-seat Elite i inter-deck body on Volvo B11R chassis. The first of these coaches, in a special livery to commemorate ten years of megabus, was exhibited at the Euro Bus Expo show in November 2012 and was entered in the April 2013 UK Coach Rally at Alton Towers. ALAN MILLAR

Stagecoach directly operates several Scottish Citylink services. Here, a Plaxton Panther-bodied Volvo B12B of Stagecoach Bluebird leaves Edinburgh for Inverness. COLIN DOUGLAS

coach interiors, Stagecoach began using the first of three generations of double-deck coaches from 1999.

Like easyBus, megabus offered on-line booking (initially only on-line) and low lead-in fares. From the outset, this majored on single fares starting at £1 plus a 50p booking fee, but the big difference was that Stagecoach used full-size, in some cases very high capacity vehicles, which it aimed to fill with paying passengers. Just as with budget airlines, the theory was that the cheapest fares were available to those booking first, with the operator charging a premium for the last seats just before departure. The travel business calls this yield marketing.

The first route, started in August 2003, offered a cheap alternative to the Oxford Tube, connecting less central termini (Oxpens coach park in Oxford, Gloucester Place in London) using 13-year-old Leyland Olympians imported from Hong Kong. More routes followed in Scotland a month later, again using high-capacity heavily-depreciated double-deckers, but as demand picked up and experience was gained, operation began migrating towards more conventional coaches.

Launch of a Glasgow-London service in 2004, initially with articulated coaches redeployed from regional Stagecoach Express work, was a sign of the direction megabus would take, exploiting opportunities for longer routes serving the UK capital. Several of the early routes, including Oxford-London, were given up.

One of the clever bits about yield marketing is that, besides trying to fill as many seats as possible, it also helps the operator plan where and when to deploy its vehicles. Stagecoach founder Sir Brian Souter says it is an electronic version of the way his pioneering intercity coach services operated in the 1980s, with computers doing the job that conductors did then in phoning the Perth headquarters from an intermediate town to say a southbound coach was filling close to capacity.

In typical Stagecoach fashion, megabus has grown partly with innovative high-capacity vehicles, including Neoplan and later Van Hool double-deckers, 15m Plaxton Panther-bodied tri-axle Volvo 65-seaters and most recently the 75-seat Plaxton Elite i inter-deck.

The brand has gone international, with an extensive and growing network in North America and into Europe, while a tie-up with the group's East Midland Trains business created megabusplus, with coaches from Yorkshire feeding into East Midlands Parkway station for onward travel to London. There also is megatrain, selling cheap seats on South West Trains between London and Hampshire.

Tensions are reignited

Stagecoach's revived interest in coach travel also reignited tensions with old rival Scottish Citylink. Megabus' expansion and its acquisition of the Edinburgh-Glasgow Motorvator brand from its independent founders prompted an intense fares and

A Plaxton Elite-bodied Volvo B12BT of Park's of Hamilton at the launch of Citylink Gold in Glasgow in 2010.
ALAN MILLAR

frequency battle between the two in 2004-05.

That ended in September 2005 with a joint venture between Stagecoach and ComfortDelGro, owned 35% by Stagecoach and managed by it, binding together Citylink's Scottish operations with much of megabus but retaining the two brands.

The MMC may have considered that coaches and trains competed in the same market, but its successor the Competition Commission took the opposite view and in 2006 ruled that the joint venture be broken up or diluted to reinstate the competition that had only lasted about a year, racking up losses for both parties.

Early in 2008, it agreed a deal that saw Park's of Hamilton — which continued to operate coaches under contract to the joint venture — operate four Glasgow-Aberdeen and one Edinburgh-Inverness service as its own, with coaches in Citylink blue and yellow but with Park's Motor Group fleetnames.

Two years later, the joint venture launched Citylink Gold, a premium alternative to megabus and Citylink, with Plaxton Elite-bodied Volvos and at-seat catering. Operation was subcontracted to Park's.

Further innovation the following year saw the trial launch of megabus sleeper, with depreciated articulated Volvos introduced between Glasgow and London, the coaches reconfigured with 24 beds (18 in the front, six in the back) and 24 seats (six in the front, 18 in the back).

Trying to sleep in such close proximity to so many fellow travellers in the confines of a moving coach might not appeal to existing coach users, but Stagecoach reckoned it had tapped into a new budget conscious market and in 2013 bought ten new 15m Van Hool Astromega double-deckers to provide a permanent service, branded megabusGold.

At best, the trial service broke even, but these new coaches have a higher capacity and an additional daytime role. For the night service, they have 42 beds, but in the daytime operate an extension of the Citylink Gold concept in Scotland as well as London-Plymouth/Cardiff, with 53 seats and an enhanced service.

Birth of the Levante

The new competition kept National Express on its toes, refining its network, embracing on-line booking and once again getting to grips with the standard of its coaches.

The Plaxton Expressliner moved on to later generations of the coachbuilder's body designs, but the original leasing arrangements fell by the wayside. In 2005 a new standard coach became a feature of contracts struck with almost all contractors.

This was the Caetano Levante, a wheelchair-accessible vehicle developed from a body called the Winner when the Portuguese coachbuilder unveiled it two years earlier. While the Expressliner was a variant of bodywork produced in other forms for the wider market, in the UK the Levante was a shape unique to

National Express, which required its contractors to buy or lease them initially on Volvo B12B or Scania K340 chassis; some of the Scanias were 14.1m tri-axle models with 61 seats.

From 2010, the specification changed to a Volvo B9R with an upgraded 48-seat interior that drew lessons from Alsa, the Spanish interurban coach operator that National Express had owned since 2005. A few operators — notably Stagecoach, which has continued as a contractor on some routes despite the development of megabus, and Park's of Hamilton — have Plaxton Elite-bodied B9Rs fitted out to a similar standard.

The Levante shape is no longer unique to National Express, though it accounts for the vast majority on UK roads. Caetano built a few bodies for Mercedes-Benz on its OC500 chassis, most of them for The King's Ferry, which has been a National Express subsidiary since 2007. And as newer Levantes have replaced them, early examples have migrated on to general coach work, either with their original operators or sold secondhand.

The livery introduced in 2003 had a short life, replaced from November 2007 by a new group-wide livery — for coaches, buses and trains in the UK — based on the white coach identity but with lower case fleetnames and a diagonal grey device described at its launch as 'connectors'.

At the same time, the group had another crack at the London airports market with Dot2Dot, an American-style shuttle service with demand responsive minibuses connecting Heathrow with hotels and businesses in central London. It failed and was sold off within a year.

While double-deckers — towing luggage trailers to make up for limited holds on the coaches themselves — form part of the megabus fleet mix, National Express finally gave up on them in 2009 when Park's of Hamilton replaced Neoplan Skyliners with Stagecoach-style 15m Plaxton Panther-bodied Volvo B12BTs.

In its various incarnations, National Express had blown hot and cold over double-deck coaches. The Standerwick VRLs fell from favour after one overturned on the M1 in 1974 when swerving to avoid an earlier accident, killing one passenger. Eleven years later, a Metroliner overturned on the A1(M) while attempting to avoid a stray sheep, again with one fatality aboard. The final blow fell in January 2007 when a Park's Skyliner took a bend too fast on the M4/M25 intersection near Heathrow, killing three passengers. Although the accident was down to driver error and the small Skyliner fleet was returned to service after passing mechanical checks, the coaches lived on borrowed time after that.

Greyhound comes to Britain

In nearly 40 years, National Express had held its own in a market beginning to be enlarged by effective new players, but as market leader it could class itself as the

MegabusGold was launched with ten Van Hool Astromegas with beds that convert into seats for daytime services. ANDY IZATT

The first Caetano Levantes operated initially in the 2004 National Express livery, as evidenced by this June 2007 view of an Arriva Midlands-operated Scania K340 passing through Evesham en route from Rugby to Brixham. ALAN MILLAR

From summer 2010, National Express standardised on the Volvo B9R chassis with a revised specification 48-seat Caetano Levante body incorporating grey leather upholstery. ALAN MILLAR

A Greyhound-liveried Irizar PB-bodied Scania K114 of First on the Greyhound service from Southsea and Portsmouth to London. ALAN MILLAR

British counterpart of America's Greyhound, providing the most comprehensive nationwide network.

But someone else owned the real Greyhound. Someone British. In 2007, FirstGroup had acquired United States school bus giant Laidlaw in its biggest expansion move.

Laidlaw also owned Greyhound and despite expectations to the contrary — there had been several rescue plans and ownership changes in prior decades — it kept Greyhound and looked at ways of improving and developing the brand.

While Stagecoach's UK bus business is substantially interurban, First's is rooted primarily in cities and large towns. Consequently it operated fewer coaches, though there were notable exceptions like the Reading-Heathrow RailAir service inherited from NBC and never part of National Express. There also was a Cardiff-Swansea Shuttle and a range of National Express contracts.

In September 2009 it launched a UK version of Greyhound. Same iconic livery, just as in the movies. Catchy American names for the coaches like *Peggy Sue* and *Billie Jean* and a lavish refit that added legroom and plush leather seats to some Irizar PB-bodied Scanias operated originally for National Express. While Greyhound had a reputation back home as the transport of last resort for those unable to afford a car or a flight, the romantic movie image worked in its favour in the UK.

Just as easyBus had begun by talking of a service to Birmingham, there had been hints of premium services with longer intercity routes radiating out of London, but the launch service was more modest: budget fare services linking Southampton and Portsmouth with London. These competed against National Express and Stagecoach's megatrain.

It followed this by rebranding the Swansea-Cardiff Shuttle as Greyhound in 2010 and in January 2011 did the same to an overnight Glasgow-London route acquired a couple of years earlier from an independent. The south coast services were extended to Bournemouth for a while, but that was as good as it got. They and the Glasgow service were axed in 2012, the south coast coaches being redeployed to Wales to extend the sole surviving service to Bristol Airport from March 2013.

With a bigger job to do in injecting new life into its bus operations, First's management cannot afford to divert precious management time to such a small part of its business. Greyhound may finally have come to a small part of Britain, but it is its emulators who dominate express coach travel this side of the Atlantic.

THE
great days
OF GⱮⱮT

JOHN ROBINSON illustrates a selection of vehicles from the varied fleet of the Greater Manchester PTE.

Under local government reorganisation the South East Lancashire North East Cheshire PTE, Selnec, became the Greater Manchester PTE, trading as Greater Manchester Transport, from 1 April 1974. The Selnec livery of orange and white was retained but a slightly darker shade of orange and a lighter white were introduced. The fleetname comprised a double M logo (called the M-blem) with the words Greater Manchester Transport alongside. On half-cab double-deckers it was planned that the M-blem and wording would be displayed in a different style to that used on more modern buses, although only a handful of former Manchester and Stockport Leyland Titans received this layout before it was abandoned in favour of the standard form. Amongst them was 5856 (HJA 956E), the first of a batch of 15 Neepsend-bodied Leyland Titan PD2/40s new to Stockport in 1967, but seen here after transfer to Oldham. It is standing in the town's bus station in the curiously-named Mumps on 3 September 1974 operating service 429 from Stamford Road to Hollinwood. The scene has now changed considerably and the railway and roundabout in the background have gone to be replaced by a new tram line, part of the expanding Metrolink, crossing the road on the level.

ABOVE: **A particular rarity in the fleet was attractive Weymann-bodied Albion Nimbus 6082 (RJX 258). New to Halifax Joint Committee in 1963, it was sold to Warrington Corporation in 1965, in turn passing to Ramsbottom Urban District Council in 1968 where it was used on the infrequent service to Holcombe Village which required a small bus. It is seen at the depot in Stubbins Lane, Ramsbottom, GMT's smallest, on 9 March 1975. Withdrawal came the following year whilst the depot closed in 1978 and operations transferred to Bury.**

BELOW: **Crook Street depot yard, Bolton, was a collection point for withdrawn buses, usually from the former Selnec Northern Division fleets of Bolton, Bury, Leigh, Ramsbottom and Rochdale. However, on 1 February 1975, the main subject of interest was in-service ex-Bolton Leyland Atlantean/East Lancs 6767 (HWH 267F), one of 15 new in 1967, which had been overturned for recovery training. The windscreen had been removed to prevent damage under the stresses incurred, but otherwise the vehicle appeared intact and afforded an excellent view of its underside, not normally seen so clearly. On the left of the picture can be seen four withdrawn buses with ex-Leigh lowbridge Leyland Titan PD2/20 6950 (WTE 24) and Dennis Loline III 6965 (268 WTE), dating from 1955 and 1961 respectively and both bodied by East Lancs, flanked by ex-Rochdale Weymann-bodied AEC Regent Vs.**

ABOVE: **The most modern double-deckers inherited from North Western were Daimler Fleetlines with lowheight Alexander bodywork. The very first, 1 (YJA 1), new in 1963, stands in Wallshaw Street depot, Oldham, still in North Western livery, on 9 April 1975. Alongside is former Oldham Corporation Leyland Atlantean 5179 (SBU 179G), one of a batch of five, new in 1969, which were the operator's first one-man operated Atlanteans, having dual-doorway bodywork by Roe to this design specified by Oldham, but with the destination indicator in a much lower position than hitherto so the driver could change the blinds from the cab.** North Western had its own premises in the town, having opened in 1966 a new garage and bus station in Clegg Street (replacing an older garage in Crofton Street) which continued to be used after the transfer of operations to Selnec Cheshire. However, when the latter was dissolved in May 1973 and the remaining former North Western buses were absorbed by the Central and Southern divisions of Selnec, its vehicles were transferred to Wallshaw Street although Clegg Street remained in use as a coach station for about another year.

ABOVE: **Ten Scania-powered MCW Metropolitan integrals joined the fleet in 1974 and were allocated to the depot at Ashton-under-Lyne which, along with those at Stalybridge and Glossop, carried the TE (Tameside) depot code. Purchased to operate principally on the Stockport to Bolton Trans-Lancs Express service 400, they were notoriously heavy on fuel and had to refuel at Stockport during their working day until they could be fitted with larger fuel tanks. As the basic off-peak requirement was for four vehicles they were also used on local services. The last of the batch, 1434 (GNC 286N), heads along Crickets Lane towards Ashton bus station, with its home depot in Mossley Road beyond the trees on the far right, operating local service 331 Smallshaw Circular, on 9 April 1975.** The livery layout was modified to suit the body mouldings which led to the orange skirt being extended up to the lower-deck waist rail with the M-blem in white. As well as their high fuel consumption the Metropolitans suffered from body corrosion leading to the entire batch being withdrawn in 1982 after a shorter than average service life.

LEFT: **Wigan Corporation became part of the GMT fleet on its inception on 1 April 1974. Entirely Leyland, and bodied in the town by either Massey or Northern Counties, the distinctive Massey bodies provided a new profile for the orange and white livery. On 29 September 1978 3233 (HJP 1), one of four Leyland Titan PD3A/2s new in 1962, climbs Ormskirk Road, Pemberton, a stone's throw from the Massey works, which by then was part of Northern Counties and producing large quantities of GMT Standards. Wigan's unique green marker lights, flanking the destination indicator and enabling the town's ratepayers to distinguish their buses at night from those of competitors, became redundant under GMT and are painted over. GMT continued operating 3233, and similar bus 3230, until 1981 by which time it was the only PTE still operating half-cab double-deckers; the last half-cabs in the fleet, former Stockport PD3s, finished in May 1982.**

ABOVE: **Seven Mancunians dominate this view inside Northenden (NN) depot on the evening of 6 January 1980, with Park Royal-bodied Daimler Fleetlines 2028 (HVM 828F) and 2072 (LNA 272G) nearest the camera. Building commenced on this garage in 1939, when new premises were required to house vehicles used on routes to Wythenshawe, a massive housing estate to the south of Manchester started in the 1920s. Construction of the garage progressed well, but it was requisitioned in its part-finished state by the Ministry of Aircraft Production when war broke out. However, not all the building was required and when the pit area was completed in November 1941 Manchester Corporation was allowed to use that section and some of the large outdoor parking area, which was equipped with steam heating to keep bus radiators warm at night. Construction then ceased and it was only completed and fully handed over in January 1946. The main garage area had wide concrete spans providing an unobstructed parking area free of pillars; it closed in October 1986 at the start of deregulation, although for a few months afterwards was used to store withdrawn buses. It is now used by an airport parking company.**

LEFT: **Also acquired from North Western were 30 Bristol RELLs with Alexander Y-type bodies. New in 1970, these attractive buses served GMT until 1981-82. Princess Road-based 332 (NJA 332H) stands in the darkness of Chorlton Street coach station, Manchester, operating a Sunday evening short-working of service 232 to Bramhall Village on 8 April 1979. Formerly service 32, operated jointly by North Western and Manchester Corporation Transport, which ran from Lower Mosley Street bus station to Middlewood, it was re-located to Chorlton Street upon the closure of Lower Moseley Street in May 1973 being, at the time of this photograph, the only GMT service to use this rather inhospitable fume-filled site beneath a multi-storey car park.**

ABOVE: **Lancashire United Transport was taken over by the PTE on 1 January 1976 but retained its identity and original fleet numbers, even though many clashed with numbers allocated to GMT buses. It had standardised on 33ft-long Daimler Fleetlines with Northern Counties bodywork for its double-deck requirements from 1971 to 1974, building up a fleet of 16. 361 (ATJ 275J), from the first batch of six, stands just inside the entrance at Atherton depot after running through the bus wash ready to take up a peak hour working on service 551 from Leigh to Warrington on 5 November 1980. Ex-LUT Guy Arab V/Northern Counties trainer TV6 (515 VTB), in the yellow and white livery introduced the previous year for the training fleet, appears slightly blurred as it moves towards the camera during the time exposure required to obtain this picture.**

ABOVE: **Although the standard GMT single-deck livery was white with an orange skirt and roof, none of the ex-LUT vehicles received this layout. Various layouts were tried including that seen on Plaxton Derwent-bodied Seddon RU 390 (DTC 738J) parked outside the Merseyside PTE depot in Hall Street, St Helens, on 24 May 1980. LUT was a large customer of Seddon and purchased a total of 50 RUs in 1970-71 with this style of bodywork which was also used on 30 of its Bristol REs. All-over orange eventually became the standard GMT livery for this body style. In this view the bus defiantly retains its red LUT wheels and is devoid of a fleetname whilst surprisingly the metal trim around the wheelarches has not been painted over.**

RIGHT: **Following the closure of Ramsbottom, GMT's smallest depot became that at Glossop, in Derbyshire, inherited from North Western, which had about 20 vehicles. Climbing Dinting Road, operating the 392 Glossop Circular on 18 November 1980, is very lightly-loaded Northern Counties-bodied Leyland Fleetline standard 8021 (ANA 21T), carrying a TE depot code, Glossop being classed as a sub-depot of Tameside which by this time was at new site in Whitelands Road, Ashton-under-Lyne, opened in November 1977, replacing the former municipal depots at Ashton and Stalybridge.**

ABOVE: **Thirteen of the then advanced Metro-Scanias, all of two-door layout, were acquired by Selnec in 1972-73, the first four of which were allocated to Bolton along with four Leyland Nationals for comparative purposes. At this time all were numbered in the EX experimental fleetnumber series. The Leyland National eventually won the day and during 1976 the Metro-Scanias were all concentrated at Leigh. 1350 (VVM 605L) is passing the entrance to Warrington Central railway station as it heads along Winwick Street for the bus station on 17 February 1981. It is operating service 587 (formerly Leigh Corporation 47) which ran from Leigh to Warrington via Croft; sister service 586 (formerly Leigh Corporation 46) ran between the two towns via Padgate. As with the Metropolitans, the application of the livery respected the polished mouldings of these buses, resulting in a deeper orange skirt than on any previous vehicles.**

ABOVE: **Oldham-based Leyland National 147 (JNA 603N), one of 70 new in 1975, climbs up Shaw Hall Bank Road past Greenfield railway station on 2 September 1981, operating service 355 from Oldham to Ashton-under-Lyne. At the time of this photograph the 355 went through Greenfield village and turned at the Clarence Hotel to come back again, explaining why it is travelling in the opposite direction to Ashton at this point. These vehicles were released from the Leyland National plant in Workington in plain white and went to Northern Counties in Wigan for the orange to be added prior to entering service.**

LEFT: **Heading along Bolton Road, Hawkshaw, on 1 May 1981 operating service 565 from Edgworth to Bury is 6038 (KKV 700G), a Willowbrook-bodied Daimler Fleetline which was new in 1968 as a Daimler demonstrator. It was purchased by Rochdale Corporation, but delivered direct to Selnec, in Rochdale livery, in 1970 where it joined four similar vehicles purchased by Rochdale in 1968, although with single-doorway rather than the dual-doorway of 6038. This service had formerly been operated by Ribble as its 255 but in April 1974 a small number of Ribble services operating within the PTE area in Bolton and Bury were transferred to GMT, including this one which was initially numbered 483 before it became 565. All five of these Fleetline saloons were withdrawn by the end of 1981.**

LEFT: **Two non-standard double-deckers were delivered in March 1983. These were Scania BR112DHs with Northern Counties bodywork and were allocated to Leigh, which already had experience of the Metro-Scanias, the survivors of which were still in service there although all would be withdrawn by October of that year. A shallower panel above the windscreen, due to the high driving position, prevented these buses from having GMT's standard destination layout, illustrated by 1461 (FWH 461Y) leaving Leigh bus station on 5 June 1983 operating the 594 circular. This service, formerly Leigh Corporation 4, had previously run to the ominously-named Dangerous Corner but became a circular along with service 593 (formerly to Hindley Green and ex-Leigh Corporation 3) running in the opposite direction. These buses carried the new livery of orange, brown and white which had been adopted at the end of 1980.**

RIGHT: **Two Kassbohrer Setra S215HD integrals were delivered to the PTE's Charterplan coach operation in January 1983. Numbered 30 and 31, they carried registration numbers 515 VTB and 583 TD respectively, transferred from ex-LUT Guy Arab training buses (515 VTB appears in the background in an earlier photo) which were re-registered BNC 988/9B. This Setra was the National Coach Rally Coach of the Year 1983, as evidenced by the surprisingly modest lettering at the top of the windscreen in this view at the Little Roodee coach park, Chester on 13 July 1983. Two more Setras joined the fleet in October that year.**

LEFT: **The final 60 chassis of GMT's last Leyland Atlantean order, which would have taken the fleet numbers for PTE standards up to 8825, was cancelled and replaced by one for 60 Olympians. The first 25 of these started to arrive at the end of 1982 and featured Leyland's automatic Hydracyclic gearbox. However, for comparison purposes ten buses (3026-35) were ordered with Voith gearboxes and also had the high driving position. Split equally between Princess Road and Hyde Road garages 3028 (A28 ORJ) from the former is seen passing beneath the electrified railway line from Manchester Piccadilly to Crewe in Kirkmanshulme Lane, Longsight, on 31 March 1985. It is operating the so-called circular 53 route which ran around the southern and eastern suburbs of Manchester from Old Trafford to Cheetham Hill but was not actually a complete circle.**

Soul

ROBERT E. JOWITT, with many years behind him of driving his own or other people's buses, and with descriptions of epic journeys long or short to illustrate his argument, embarks on the contentious issue of whether or not buses have souls.

Sprightly Paris Renault TN4H 3422, a Jowitt fancy with those divine French 2s in the fleet number, in the Rue de Rennes in April 1970.

"Pourquoi as-tu fait ca?" she demanded of me quite plainly. "Why did you do that?" There were no words to hear, but the message, by extra-sensory-perception or whatever it may be, came to me clearly enough. I had just clipped the rear nearside wheel of my 1936 Renault Paris bus 3380 against a mildly obtrusive kerbstone on a sharpish corner of the Kingston by-pass; she was not unreasonable in making protest. This was back in the early 1970s when, as cognoscenti know, I had lately started on my career of Parisian preservation; and it had soon become apparent to me that these buses could speak their mind, respond to me and my treatment of them, let me know for sure when they were in a bad mood.

Cynics may argue that even dogs and cats, though adoring of their master, cannot have a soul in the same way as a human being, and therefore all the more the argument that mere buses certainly cannot. On the other hand people who love their vehicles may well agree with me, buses can be just as angelic or foul-tempered as the best of girl-friends or wives... and inform you in equally expressive terms.

The story of my love for and purchase of Paris buses has been told often enough to need no repetition, save here to say that while I never had any doubt that among the TN4Fs 3267 would be my choice, there was more than one option in my mind for the TN4Hs. Included were 3339, the second-oldest of the whole batch and a rather charming number, and 3422, a bus which when you rode on her managed to exude a lot of character; diverse fates (3339 was bagged by a Swedish museum – is she still there? – and 3422 went to disposal before I had my act together) caused me in the end to select another hot favourite, 3380... which must have been meant, for she was soon as close to me as was 3267. I must add that the number of a bus can for me add to its delight; three threes are nine is obvious, and 3422 boasted twice-fold those gorgeous French 2s which look like nines, but it is not just numbers which give forth good vibrations. (And this is a term liable to misinterpretation in the context of Parisian streets or their surfaces).

At this date I had just returned to reside in Winchester, where I had spent my childhood and teenage years and now, more sympathetic to buses than in the Southern steam era, I developed a belated (very, as sadly it was to prove) affection for the King Alfred Motor Services. Among the charmingly varied fleet my favourites were the three 1959 Leyland Tiger Cubs 103, 104 and 105, and of these, though they were to all intents and purposes identical, 103 was for me the best; if I sighted one of them coming from afar off I knew, by some magic instinct, when it was going to be 103. I was almost invariably right!

My abortive rescue attempt of 103 is another of those oft repeated tales, and other failures have been related elsewhere, thought I might add that these included the fantastic Bilbao ex-London trolleybus-converted-to-diesel 277, this number having the merit of applying, in Hymns Ancient & Modern, to Nearer my God to Thee; which might have proved all too appropriate for so titanic a vehicle!

Further familiar stories from 40 years of bus-inspired autobiography relate stage carriage and schools in Herefordshire, with Primrose of Leominster and Teme Valley, but a list of fairly boring Fords and Bedfords, fond though I grew of some of them despite here and there defects, might prove

as boring as the coaches themselves. Suffice a few words on one of my regulars, the one I loved best, Teme Valley FUJ 917V. Banal in retrospect I must tell how, brief as the elopement proved, I stole her! It was a booked and therefore no-tacho run to drop some kids at some scientific spot west of Hereford, and pick them up three hours later. I could have sat in FUJ outside the gate, but surely I was justified in taking her just down the road to look for a sandwich. Not just down the road, but over the ridge and down to Vowchurch and mile after mile of the pastoral paradise of the Golden Valley. No one knew where I was, probably no one cared anyway, and FUJ was all mine to take her whither I would, on and on. We were companions, joyfully united. I took her in truth to not far short of Hay-on-Wye, where I decided I had really best turn back... probably not above 30 miles in all, but all rapturous! I never found a sandwich.

The sceptic may argue that this impression of rapport is brought about simply by prolonged familiarity, but I move on – with family upheaval – from Herefordshire to the Isle of Wight where, becoming a casual driver for Southern Vectis I can relate three tales which to my mind disprove this notion and justify and enhance, perchance, that the character or indeed soul – or lack of it – of the individual bus is the vital issue.

Southern Vectis was in due time swallowed by Go Ahead, which later brought me a summons for a task across the water, this providing the first of the tales I have promised.

The duty was to take ten Optares from Biddulph, Staffs, to Blandford, Dorset, or from what I took to be a dealer to a depot in the village of Pimperne where the Optares would work on schools for Wilts & Dorset or Damory. The crew, mostly SV office staff, set out at break of dawn from Newport in a minibus, and soon a count revealed we were one driver short. My son John was accordingly telephoned, and dug out of bed and taken off his Vectis school run to drive post-haste to Cowes for the Fast-Cat to park, and catch us up (we crawling slowly across the Solent on the car-ferry) at Southampton, where the last two drivers, W&D men, also joined us. That minibus was about the most uncomfortable wretch I have ever encountered, the A34 and the M40 did not look their best. At the end of the M6 Toll the girl in the booth kindly informed us that a tanker was overturned further up the M6 so we pulled off for a mystery tour of the south-west fringes of Cannock Chase. Well, I received the impression that our driver was mystified, but it wasn't for casual me, even with a map, to question his wisdom in where he was going. In the distance we saw the tailback and then, crossing the M6, actually glimpsed the wreck.

Ancient and modern: a 1936 Paris Renault TN4F, second oldest of the entire series, passing the ORTF (French Radio and Television HQ) in September 1970.

Rescue seemed to be proceeding apace. We rejoined the motorway and observed it was tailing back southbound as well... but we trusted it would be clear before we came back down.

In due time the unmistakable shape of Mow Cop clove the horizon four miles east of us, when we turned off to pass through Congleton, Mow Cop was three miles south of us though we could no longer see it, and nor could we when it was about a mile west of us as we sat-navved to our Biddulph destination and ten awaiting anonymous white Optares.

All the way up our Chris had been murmuring to himself at intervals what sounded like Biddula, or perhaps Biddulfa, or even Budolf. What we saw of the place was hardly meritorious.

We had discussed the route to Blandford. A computer print-out suggested going through the middle of Bath, and here I had to speak up to protest against the folly of such a course with a convoy of ten buses. It transpired that I knew the southern part of the route – avoiding Bath – better than anyone else professed to, so it was agreed I should lead from the Strensham services on the M5 while our Steve would lead on the northern section, with which he stated he was familiar. So with route decided and take-over formalities concluded we set out from Biddulph at about 3 o'clock for our 200-mile trek.

As far as Congleton we kept station, Steve holding back after lights or roundabouts for stragglers to catch up. In Congleton heavy traffic and a cloudburst brought serious gaps. Just before the M6, in a stormy gleam of sunlight, I had a sight of the whole Cheshire plain spread out north-west. Immediately on the M6 the only bus I could now see ahead of me turned off into Sandbach services. Well, it was a case of every man for himself, and I kept going; later I discovered his bus was laden with mineral water bottles, some empty, some still full. I suppose that's one way of coping with a doubtful radiator.

Some way further south I came up with the southbound tail-back, by no means dispersed. Crawl and crawl, until at length I saw, in the distance, Optares turn off for Stafford. I did likewise, and stopped for a call and a study of the map... and thanked heaven that I had brought one! By now the others were lost to me, and of course every second motorist on the M6 had thought of Stafford. Our Marc said afterwards he had stuck to the motorway and speeded his passage by coming off at slip-exits and rejoining beyond, thus bypassing long sections of queue; I believe he arrived first at Pimperne! Once, in Stafford, I saw my leaders but lost them again and followed my own route south to beyond the wreck, where I rejoined the M6. Now the appalling tailback was northbound and I reflected upon the madness of the human race in its dependence on the frail motor.

This madness persisted on my right hand side down to beyond the junction of the M6 and the M5 where, on the hard shoulder, I halted behind half a dozen Optares... Steve's was pouring out smoke, he said. We couldn't stay where we were, rush hour impending,

1936 Renault TN4H 3395 at the Palais Royal in 1970 shows how desirable these buses were.

Beauty in the Broadway. Jowitt's favourite King Alfred Tiger Cub 103 in Winchester, about 1972, mini-skirt era still prevailing.

Steve would push on in hope, and the rest assemble at Frankley services for necessary break and planning. Frankley is amongst the most horrid of service areas, I decided. We lined up five Optares. One W&D man came in but pushed on. Steve was presumed ahead, the rest anywhere. To the west I could see the Clent Hills, much featured in the Black Country novels of Francis Brett Young, one of the great British novelists vastly popular in the earlier years of the 20th century but now alas largely forgotten save by a few devotees such as Jowitt. Over foulburgers I now, henceforth as leader, explained firmly, with my map, how we would come off at junction 11A onto the A417 and then at Cirencester off the A417 and over it for the A429. What simpler... but I repeated it. Sue said she would pull through Strensham services to see if Steve had failed there, and catch us up beyond Birdlip at an agreed lay-by. So with four now behind me I struck south.

The Worcestershire countryside smiled green in brilliant intervals between rainstorms, wonderful lighting which of course I could not photograph. Westward the teeth of the Malverns rose, to me a dearer and fairer range than any Pyrenee or Swiss Alp, then east hove up Housman's beloved Bredon (albeit we were rather late for summertime) and we were in the heart of John Moore's Blue Field and Elmbury territory. Goodness, how he, who deplored the cruelties of progress, would have hated this savage roaring motorway scar through his heartland! Sue, as planned, fell out from the column, and we other

four turned off onto the A417. Up and beyond Birdlip (our Optares tackled the grade bravely enough!) we were graced by possibly the most glorious rainbow I ever have witnessed. Sue afterwards (for it was still there when she passed) asked me exactly where its end fell, as if she wanted to search for a crock of gold, but it moved along the verge of the A417 and was quite likely over those hidden political bunkers which are alleged to be buried in that part of the Cotswolds. We duly stopped in my chosen lay-by and, despite our frantic gesticulations, Sue shot past us. We went on, and soon sighted her bus in the next Little Chef car park. Knowing it of old from small children's stops I was not inclined to take four Optares into its cramped confines, Sue could catch us up, she had her instructions.

I and my three duly turned off and over the A417 at Cirencester for the south-westwards A429. Here, reader, study your road atlas (if you have not already so done). I admit I may have misjudged the case, but I did not fancy the difficulties of Marlborough and

Jowitt's dearly beloved Teme Valley FUJ 917V, here in the Carding Mill Valley, Shropshire, in 1998.

Salisbury quite apart from that such route was too far round compared with the direct Chippenham and Warminster. We were soon in Wiltshire, with gathering darkening evening threatening.

Before Shaftesbury I viewed to the west the entire Blackmore Vale stretched under a furious grey and silver tempestuous remains of sunset. We were in Thomas Hardy country. Daylight died away. Ah, poor Tess!

It was, I guess, 40 years since I had last driven between Shaftesbury and Blandford, and had somewhat forgotten the road's nature or its potential unsuitability for an Optare convoy. Once on a ferocious zig-zag was a dead badger on our half of the road but we all four boasted afterwards that despite its being already dead we had all missed it. At last, well over six hours since we had quitted Budolf, I and my faithful three rolled in darkest shades of night into the Pimperne yard. One of the three, son John, was kind enough to congratulate me on having done excellently on the piloting.

Marc and a W&D were in before us, and Steve, despite smoke, soon after. I think the other W&D had been bidden continue to Poole. Ages later Chris, with Sue behind him, hustled in. Chris, spotting Sue at the Little Chef, had her follow him, but failed at Cirencester to cross the A417 and went 20 miles the wrong way northwards to Stow-on-the-Wold before guessing something was wrong. They came back, unlike me, via Salisbury, with Chris's foot flat on the gas thereafter on the long straights, terrifying Sue...

Pimperne proved to show, in the murk, some ex-Southern Vectis Leyland Olympians, now in new colours on local schools. Splendid buses, I had undoubtedly driven some of them even when they had been passed out but borrowed back, at the Island Bestival. I had even, with a friend, thought about buying one off Southern Vectis, but at nine grand we decided no. I bade farewell to my Optare, however, without regrets. I had done over six hours with her, and 200 miles, and, if uncomfortable, she was well behaved and dutiful enough, but no response, no soul. Or did she have a soul and, realising that I disliked and despised Optares, declined to reveal it... the very refusal perhaps indeed revealing!

The booked Southampton ferry passage was long gone, but we just caught the last boat from Lymington...

Back on the island, the next adventure was on articulated – or so-nicknamed bendy buses. For half a century I have cherished these in continental form, though more recently (even if with a sneaking

Anonymous Optares awaiting collection from Biddulph, autumn 2011.

admiration) deemed them uncouthly alien and misplaced in the streets of London. Mayor Boris Johnson evidently thought likewise and evicted them, and Southern Vectis picked up a dozen to join the special events fleet, i.e. for the Isle of Wight Festival. Candidates for learning to drive them were invited; how could I refuse? Provided you have eyes in the back of your head it's not too difficult. I was passed as OK.

The great day came; actually 21 June 2012. On service bus to the Festival site and then on John's just-off-schools to Ryde depot there were already such queues as suggested matters were awry. John and I started checking my artic, 9213, at 9.30, then, mis-adventureless, I took her to Ryde Esplanade to load, and was away by 10.30. I drove my merry ravers some three miles, then encountered the rear of a tail-back. Over the next three hours I had moved on a mile, with my mob, starting to become bored, constantly in and out for fags and hedges, and by two by two or more, gradually deserting me to walk. John, ahead, managed to turn his coach at the Fishbourne lights, aided by police, to return to Ryde and go for his schools. I had no prospect of turning an artic, and within another hour and a few hundred yards later the doors failed on me, refusing to shut, so I could not move. Police passing the other way bade me turn on my hazard lights. You do what the boys in blue tell you, yes. By the time I had shifted my few remaining faithful onto another bus edging past me in the queue my battery was flat. The greatest disappointment in my bus driving career was when the police headed a convoy of buses down the wrong side of the road to overtake the jam, and invited me to join on the end and alas, of course, I could not! The rescue I had summoned by mobile from the works took four hours via another

Testing London's cast-off bendy-buses for size, for the IW Festival tin-sheet bus station, round a derelict supermarket car park at Ryde, March 2012.

breakdown and total gridlock to reach me. Meanwhile the scene looked like descriptions of the exodus of civilians from Paris at the fall of France in 1940, the endless unmoving line of cars and buses, the bunches of heavily burdened pedestrians trudging through the rain. Smoking mildly against the rules in the useless door of 9213 – I wasn't going to stand outside and get wet – I heard from school kids tramping bus-less or mothers fetching infants having simply abandoned their cars on verges, that the trouble had started with campsite gates not ready to be opened by staff when the first punters turned up and then, when they were opened, the cars getting bogged down in the mud. The law decided this was too dangerous and the increasing quantity of cars off the ferries soon brought the entire north-east of the island to a standstill. The Fishbourne ferry terminal became so full with arrivals unable to move that subsequent ferries could

not land and had to wait tossing about in the Solent. I wondered if the passengers were singing Nearer my God to Thee. It has been argued that the Festival organisers and the police, well aware of rain-soaked jubilee and cancellations of other recent events and the known proclivities of the Festival fields for rapid transformation into mire and swamp, might have been better prepared.

My rescue came, and with copious advice on how delicately to manipulate the door buttons and how not at any price to stall or cut the engine, I was on my way. Another two or three hours, the shades of night were falling fast and I was three quarters of a mile further along and shivering with exhaustion. My dear John bucked a few rules and came out with his car. I took his car and he took 9213 back to the yard.

Compared with Budolf this was some four miles in 12 hours. At least I could boast that I had driven an artic, but even with so long a companionship she was very uncommunicative. Under the circumstances I can't really blame her.

Next day – when the night-long-continuing of the gridlock had at last been dissipated – I was somewhat relieved to be on PVLs and other double-deck heroines of antiquity rather than artics, for I was still fairly shattered. Towards evening and the end of my shift, after a day of average plodding to Cowes or Ryde, I was bidden "Take that blue one to Yarmouth." That blue one was 4835, in SV version of Moss Motors colours, usually on schools, ex-Metrobus (Crawley) Volvo Olympian, named Goose Rock. (Sad to tell SV is now abandoning the charming practice of naming buses after local coastal features.) Behind the Moss logo there must have been a tattered blind with such

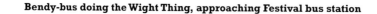

Bendy-bus doing the Wight Thing, approaching Festival bus station

A shoe-box, perhaps, but what a character! 4835, in Moss IW livery, ex-Metrobus Volvo Olympian, at Ryde depot saying to the author "Save me!"

evocative destinations as "Upper Warlingham Stn", last vestige of London Transport's once vast Country Bus empire.

Yarmouth is a good run, agreeably curvaceous and slightly undulating, across the empty country of north-west of Wight, mostly broad roads, towards evening and sunset, nearly free of traffic. I gave 4839 all I could give her, and she responded magnificently, plainly loving it, swinging into the bends and tackling the grades under my foot hard down with absolute joie-de-vivre. I cannot say I broke the speed limit, but I might well have done. At Yarmouth I gathered the last of the ferry stragglers and sped back in the same style. Heaven, I thought, I will never have another bus-drive as good as this, I would gladly have dropped out thereafter with this turn as the glorious finale.

Naturally, in subsequent days, it did not work out thus, but at the Festival some of my passengers, who must have caught the spirit of the trip, thanked me heartily for a grand run.

A couple of days later I saw 4835 sitting in Ryde yard, took some photos, and she said to me, in pourquoi as tu fait ca mode, "Buy me, buy me!" Verily the Festival was likely to be almost the final fling for these buses, for when the last of their schools were done at end of term a few weeks later they were due for withdrawal, heading for sale or even scrapping. I couldn't afford such anyway, though, quite futilely, adding 48 and 35 to my lottery ticket numbers.

Some weeks later I chanced by Ryde again, and she said "Save me, save me!" Would I could, but I was soon to commence dispersing my Paris fleet to the younger generation, what possibly could I want with a probably well-worn and – to me – quite modern and rather ugly shoe-box.

Nevertheless, if ever there was love at first sight – and I have experienced it more than once, if ending in tears, with the fair sex – this bus 4835 and I shared it. There was, however, utterly no prospect of my hearing her say, in some future, if I kerbed her, "Pourquoi, etc" or rather, given her origins, in perky Surrey tongue, "Whotcher do that fer!" No, impossible bus, though a friend in a high place won me her blind!

But for sure, like those I loved so well for so long, and still love now, 4835 had a soul!

Hull's spectacular avant-garde livery particularly suited the Corporation's unique Roe-bodied Sunbeam MF2B trolleybuses. They had two doors and two staircases for future one-man-operation, but such use never came about. There were 16, and they were the city's last new trolleybuses.

The thrill of BLUE BUSES

Blue was never the most widely-used colour for bus liveries, but it's a favourite of **TONY GREAVES.**

All photographs by the author.

I have always preferred blue-liveried buses, which is not to say I don't like red, green or maroon ones - I just think that you can't beat a bus wearing a dignified and classy blue livery, and such buses often happened to be owned by a small municipality. This ideal came a little unstuck for me with the introduction of some of the plasticky shades of modern times, further

compromised by the introduction of diagonal stripes. We now have ghastly multiple shades of pastel colours which at the moment are usually and thankfully clean. My traditional tastes may surprise some given that I am a graphic artist and have always worked in the world of advertising.

We seemed to be blessed with many blue-liveried operators in Yorkshire up to the 1970s. I can credit my granddad with starting my interest in buses as he used to take me for walks around Scarborough in my pre-school years. Our first call was usually the Wallace Arnold parking area to the rear of St. Columba's church, after which we looked at the West Yorkshire bus station on Northway. I much later discovered that this was the only such building to be opened during World War 2. From there we went on to the Westwood bus station, the Scarborough base of the indigo blue and primrose buses of East Yorkshire. The buildings on the island platform matched the buses in that they were faced in blue and primrose tiles, finished off with the

TOP: **A Samuel Ledgard ex-Preston Corporation PD1 with an Alexander-built Leyland body at Horsforth New Road en route to Ilkley via Otley. This bus still exists and is undergoing extensive restoration. A Leeds City Transport Titan is in the background.**

MIDDLE: **An East Yorkshire fully-fronted Leyland Titan PD2/Roe former coach is seen between duties in Hull on t'muck (really, that was the overspill bus park's name), alongside a Willowbrook-bodied AEC Regent V. The Titan was new in 1952 and was withdrawn in 1967.**

BOTTOM: **An ex-London Transport RT in the Ledgard's fleet approaches Otley bus station, on the Harrogate to Bradford route. The grey edging to the wheels was an Otley depot feature. Ledgard had almost 40 ex-London RTs.**

The author's favourite Bradford trolleybuses were the third-hand BUT 9611Ts of 1949, which had been new to Darlington Corporation. Doncaster acquired them in the late 1950s, then in 1960 when they passed to Bradford, where they were rebodied with handsome East Lancs bodies with deep windscreens and a small front overhang.

LEFT: **Ashton-under-Lyne Corporation** was one of the original 11 municipalities absorbed by the Selnec PTE in 1969, but its blue livery continued to be seen for several years. Ashton was one of those municipalities that would not accept advertising on its buses.

RIGHT: **Lytham St. Annes Corporation Transport became Fylde Borough Transport as a result of local government reorganisation in 1974. This Leyland PD2/Orion wears the new name, and the livery application helps the unbalanced appearance of the body.**

ABOVE: **Doncaster independent Blue Ensign was well known for the excellent presentation of its small fleet. This Roe-bodied AEC Regent V was typical, with polished paintwork and wheel trims.**

ABOVE: **Despite attempts to disguise the very ugly lines of its Alexander body with Southend Corporation's attractive blue and cream, this Albion Lowlander still looks a visual mess, says the photographer. It is seen in Windsor working for Alder Valley which was short of buses.**

underlined company fleetname. There was real excitement when one of the nearly new full-fronted double-deck coaches arrived. These were almost avant-garde in design, complete with high-backed seats, domed Beverley Bar roof, folding rear doors and polished metal trim. As these were mostly primrose with a little Riviera blue they should be outside the scope of this article, but several were repainted in bus livery and so may be included.

In 1962 my family (and I!) moved to Pudsey, near Leeds. Very soon I came across the Samuel Ledgard fleet, the smart blue and grey buses of which operated some of the services in Pudsey. Other services in Pudsey were provided by the always smart two-tone green buses of Leeds City Transport and the red ones of Farsley Omnibus Company and Yorkshire Woollen District.

The very smart light blue and primrose (officially primrose, but not at all like East Yorkshire's shade) buses and trolleybuses of Bradford City Transport could be seen within a short distance of Pudsey. In October 1967, when the Executors of Samuel Ledgard sold the business to the Transport Holding Company, the majority of services passed to West Yorkshire Road Car, but the Leeds-Pudsey-Bradford service became the 78, jointly operated by Leeds and Bradford City Transport departments. So, for its share, BCT's light blue and primrose replaced Ledgard's mid blue and grey. This situation continued until the advent of the West Yorkshire PTE on All Fool's Day in 1974, after which the pretty awful Verona green and Buttermilk prevailed. Not only were the colours of the livery wishy-washy, but the new operator seemed at a loss as to how to apply it, with several layout variations being tried.

I had acquired my first camera, a Halina, when I was 14 and by my early 20s I had moved on to Practika and then Pentax cameras in my constant quest to photograph buses. This urge took me to various places, from the alleged Leeds Central Bus Station – central, it isn't – to ever more distant destinations, at first on organised enthusiast trips and later, day trips with friends in a car. One weekend might be a trip to Scotland, while the next might be the South Coast or Wales.

This is a selection of personal favourites in blue liveries from trips made around the country... plus a few horrors!

Kelvin Hall SHOW

Glasgow's Kelvin Hall had a long association with the transport business. It was for many years the venue for the Scottish Motor Show, and it then housed the city's transport museum. **Billy Nicol** illustrates visiting coaches in the venue's later years.

ABOVE: **A Leyland Tiger with Duple Laser body from the Strathtay Scottish fleet is seen in 1996. It had been new to Midland Scottish in 1984.**

LEFT: **An Oban & District Leyland Leopard with Duple Dominant body awaits its passengers in 1995. The coach had been new to Alexander Midland, passing to the new independent Oban & District business in 1992. Oban & District is now part of West Coast Motors.**

ABOVE: **Alexander-bodied Leyland Tigers were bought by a number of Scottish Bus Group subsidiaries, but this most Scottish-looking coach in the Stagecoach Bluebird fleet was one of a small number bought by the National Bus Company and had been new to East Midland Motor Services.**

BELOW: **A smart Leyland Tiger with Plaxton Paramount 3200 body from the fleet of Docherty of Auchterarder heads a line of parked Plaxtons in 1993.**

LEFT: **Ayrshire independent Marbill of Beith has always operated a varied fleet. Seen in 1996, this Duple-bodied Leyland Leopard had been new to Southdown in 1978.**

RIGHT: **Ex-NBC ECW-bodied Leyland Leopards were fairly rare in Scotland. This one was operated by Essbee of Coatbridge and had been new to United Counties.**

LEFT: **An unusual B10M was this short model operated by Allander of Milngavie. It had Plaxton Bustler bodywork and had originally been used by Ralph of Langley on contracts at London's Heathrow Airport. It was new in 1986 and is seen in 2002, its age disguised by an Ulster registration mark. The Allander name comes from a local river.**

RIGHT:
MacEwan's of Amisfield, near Dumfries, was the owner of this Mercedes-Benz with Plaxton Beaver coach bodywork, seen in 1997. The coach had been new two years earlier to Glen of Port Glasgow.

LEFT: **Lochs and Glens is a high-quality tour operator which has standardised on Volvos. In 2001 this B10M with Jonckheere Mistral body was typical of the fleet. It had been new to the company in 1999.**

RIGHT: **This former London Transport DMS-type Daimler Fleetline was operated by McDade's of Uddingston. It was new in 1976 and looked well for a 22-year-old bus when photographed in 1998.**

FOR old TIMES sake

Stewart J. Brown looks at how bus timetables have changed over the years.

Until the 1960s most bus operators, large or small, issued timetable books. Some covered the entire operation, although really big operators – Ribble, for example – issued a number of area books. As well as giving bus times, they usually contained some details on the company's rules and regulations, on occasion extending to many pages of small print which, surely, nobody ever read. If they had, they would have found when travelling with the Scottish Bus Group in the 1960s, for example, that they could not "when in or on any vehicle throw any money to be scrambled for by any person on the road or footway; or throw out of the vehicle any bottle, liquid or litter or any article or thing likely to annoy persons or to cause danger or injury to any person or property". And, of course, a passenger could not "conduct himself in a riotous or disorderly manner".

The clarity of timetable information varied, and a mixture of letters and symbols could be used to indicate diversions from the main route, short workings, or buses which only operated on certain days of the week. That started to change in the 1960s, with the British Omnibus Public Relations Committee recommending a standard timetable format which was adopted by most of the big company operators from around 1965. With it came the 24-hour clock. Timetable cognoscenti may smile at the idea that this needed to be explained – but it did. Indeed, as an aside, when young ladies in the office of the bus operator I was working for at that time were told that the company was adopting the 24-hour clock they actually believed it meant they'd be working night shifts...

A debate emerging around the same time addressed the merits of big timetable books versus individual leaflets for each route or groups of routes. The big book was standard practice. Supporters argued that it let customers know the extent of the network. Opponents countered that most people were only interested in local routes so why, for example, should someone in Greenock buy a 452-page Western SMT timetable which contained information on local services in Dumfries, 90 miles away, which they were never going to use.

It took a long time for that debate to be settled, but by the mid-1980s it was clear that timetable books were on the way out. And the leaflets which replaced them were free.

Is the printed timetable under threat from new technology? Information on bus times is freely available on the internet, although not always in a user-friendly format. And a growing number of operators and local authorities offer live timetable information, accessible via assorted mobile devices.

My guess is that while demand for printed timetables will reduce, it won't disappear. I can and on occasion do check the times of my local buses on the internet – but I still keep a timetable leaflet in my desk, and that remains my first source of information. Or is that just a sign of my age....?

The selection of timetables which follows, in chronological order, was influenced solely by each operator's approach to cover design. And, as everyone knows, you can't judge a book by its cover.

....

London Coastal Coaches 1947-48
16 pages, 185x120mm. Price 2d.

....

The front cover of this London Coastal Coaches brochure shows a pretty half-cab coach passing a Dickensian-looking wayside inn. London Coastal Coaches operated Victoria Coach Station and acted as booking agents for the operators using the terminal. This isn't actually a timetable, but

instead a list of destinations in England and Wales from Aberaman to Ystrad Rhondda and Accrington to York Town (which is clearly not the same place as York as the single fare to York Town is 3s 6d (17.5p), while that to York is 19s 9d (98p)). Only a few Scottish destinations are mentioned and are marked "By SMT to Scotland".

Inside the booklet notes: "A word as to the comfort of your journey by coach in winter. It is everything that can be wished for ... the most modern luxury coaches are put into service – heated, ventilated, draught-free, comfortably upholstered, well lit up, the running as smooth as that of a high-class car, hot beverages and-or food at the recognised stopping places."

And of Victoria Coach Station it says: "It offers the traveller all amenities – tea-shop, snack bar, fully-licensed restaurant and bar. Departure hours are always a scene of great animation as huge coaches, comfortable and cosy inside, roll up into their respective bays, load, and are off on time. Crowds of eager passengers move about, loud-speakers issue their instructions, inspectors mingle with the travellers and proffer information and advice. There is the usual buzz and hum of voices; engines may be heard now and again lazily ticking over. At night, or on grey dismal days, the lighting is of thoroughly modern brilliance."

University Motor School (prospectus free on application).

After explaining that the word 'car' means omnibus or trolleybus, the passenger regulations warn: "It is an offence for any person taking or endeavouring to take any position otherwise than behind persons in a line or queue already forming or to enter or attempt to enter any car before any other person desiring to enter the same who stood in front of him or her in such queue or line."

Which is a long-winded way of saying don't jump the queue.

The Mexborough and Swinton Traction Company Limited, 1961
36 pages, 240x105mm. Price 6d

This souvenir timetable marks what at first seems a strange anniversary – 54 years of public service. But it was in fact marking the end of electric traction, initially by trams and later by trolleybuses. An introduction by the company chairman, E L Taylor, notes that 71% of

route mileage is covered by "motor omnibus services" leaving just one trunk route run by trolleybuses. He goes on: "In present day conditions the main line will be most efficiently served by double deck vehicles. This would be impossible with trolleybuses on account of over-bridges which are too low to accommodate both the vehicle and its overhead wiring; the problem can only be solved by the use of low-height double deck motor buses.

"In their forty-five

Manchester Corporation Transport, February 1952
272 pages, 135x110mm. Price 6d.

The cover of this chunky timetable shows a fairly typical Manchester bus of the time, a Crossley DD42 against a backdrop of the city's grand Victorian town hall. The 6d price on the cover of this and many of the other timetables equates to 2.5p.

The index runs from Alderley to Wythenshaw, and identifies trolleybus services with the letters 'T.B.' after the route number. Service frequencies are high, the 53, for example, from Cheetham Hill to Trafford Park, runs every 6 minutes most of the day on weekdays, rising to every 3 minutes on Saturdays and falling back to a respectable every 10 minutes on Sundays.

Advice proffered includes: "Between 7 and 9 a.m., and 5 and 6-30 p.m. The demand for transport is so great that some delay and discomfort is inevitable, even though every available vehicle is being fully utilised. If you travel other than during peak periods you will help the worker, and will be able to travel in comfort which the Department is only too glad to place at your disposal."

The timetable has a few adverts, including from Graham Bros, main dealers for Vauxhall, Bedford and Scammell, Autax Taxi (radio controlled) and Veritys

years of life the trolleybuses have served the area well, and there will be some sentimental regret to see them disappear. But there can be no doubt at all that the new motor buses which are to take their place will provide a vastly more comfortable and efficient service."

The Atlantean on the cover illustrates the new order. It was of course technically a lowbridge rather than a lowheight bus. The timetable lists just nine routes, six of which are marked as being operated jointly with Rotherham Corporation Transport Department.

Jersey Motor Transport, 1961/62
48 pages, 175x125mm. Price 4d.

A fine drawing of one of JMT's Leyland Titans features on the cover of this timetable. An odd feature is that on many services the last outward journey from St Helier is marked 'LP'. An Important Notice explains that "Services timetabled to 'Last Passenger' will run the full distance for the benefit of inward passengers, if the Depot Inspector is notified before the time of departure from the Weighbridge or Snow Hill." That it was indeed an Important Notice means that it appears on 24 of the timetable's 48 pages.

Like many other bus operators, JMT singles out dogs for special mention with the stern warning: "Dogs are carried on sufferance."

Halifax Passenger Transport, August 1965
110 pages, 110x140mm. Price 6d.

It's clearly a Northern Counties-bodied Daimler Fleetline on the cover, but with distinctly odd proportions. The indication that there's a supermarket in the background may be intended to convey modernity. And at least the artist didn't use a half-cab double-decker, a type still entering service in Halifax in the mid 1960s.

Inside, the undertaking promotes its private hire service and seeks to recruit drivers, conductors and conductresses offering holidays with pay, free uniform, free travel to and from work and a sick pay scheme.

There is no commercial advertising, but on some pages there are quaint little homilies: "Stop accidents before they stop you" and "Careless hurry means endless worry", for example.

While the route network has changed significantly in the best part of 50 years, it's good to note that now, as then, there's an hourly service between Halifax and Heptonstall. In 1965 it took 37 minutes. Today, operated by First, it takes … wait for it, exactly the same. But no longer runs on Sundays.

Aldershot & District Traction Co Ltd, 1967
212 pages, 220x135mm. Price 1s.

The cover shows an aerial view of a changing world, with buses in traditional green, most of them Dennis Lolines. This was soon to change, as Aldershot & District was merged with Thames Valley to create the red-liveried Alder Valley fleet.

The timetable uses the 24-hour clock, which was widely adopted by bus companies from 1965. It also uses standardised and easily understood codes, such as 'S' for Saturday only trips, or 'NS' for journeys which did not run on Saturdays. The only adverts are for the company's own services – "It's better going by

'Traction'" – and the offer of "superlative service" for private hire customers.

....

Huddersfield Corporation Passenger Transport, April 1967
114 pages, 150x125mm. Price 6d.

....

It might be 1967, but the cover image on this timetable looks more like 1947 with a trolleybus alongside what appears to be an AEC Regent III with its exposed radiator.

Virtually every bus timetable mentions dogs, and in Huddersfield the ruling is that "At the conductor's discretion dogs which are not of an objectionable nature may be carried on the upper deck only at half adult fare." Objectionable nature? Did conductors quiz each dog before it boarded to ensure it was a sweet natured creature?

And the word "pram" had evidently not entered Huddersfield Corporation's vocabulary. The timetables notes: "Folding Perambulators carried free subject to conductor's discretion. Cycles and large perambulators are not carried." Perambulator? Have you ever heard anyone use that word to describe a contraption for wheeling children around?

Passengers are advised that "correspondence concerning the services of the Department should be addressed to the General Manager" who had a string of letters after his name. He was E. V. Dyson, M.I.Mech.E., A.M.I.E.E., A.M.Inst.T., which no doubt impressed disgruntled passengers in Slaithwaite.

There were a few adverts for local businesses, and one from Daimler, "suppliers of High Quality Double Deck Bus Chassis to Huddersfield Corporation Transport Department".

....

Leeds City Transport, June 1968
212 pages, 165x110mm. Price 6d.

....

Only 14 months and 18 miles separate this Leeds timetable from the previous Huddersfield booklet – but what a difference. Leeds uses a modern bus on an exciting new section of the city's inner ring road. Well, it opened in 1967, and I'm sure it was still exciting in 1968. Where Huddersfield used the established 12-hour clock; Leeds used the 24-hour clock. It may not have been more easily understood but it was certainly modern.

Dogs got a good deal on Leeds buses, with a flat 2d fare and no mention of their nature. One-man operation was still a novelty, and such services carried the explanation: "All buses on this service are one-man operated. Passengers pay as they enter at the front of the bus. To help, please have your fare ready when boarding."

Leeds offered a timetable subscription service, for 5s a year. Two of the operator's vehicle suppliers advertised in the timetable, local bodybuilder Roe, and chassis supplier AEC who had some quaint ideas about the features which bus users noticed in an advert which began: "When you see 'AEC' on the wheel hub of the bus or coach in which you are about to ride you know that your journey is going to be safe, smooth and comfortable."

....

Western SMT, June 1968
452 pages, 210x135mm. Price 6d.

....

When the Scottish Bus Group adopted the new standard timetable layout in 1965 it adopted the same cover for each of its subsidiary companies, but with different background colours. All featured a representation of an Alexander Y-type.

Western's timetable included the services of some other operators, including five independents – Blue Band, Carruthers, Gibson's, Graham's and McGill's – and services operated by United from Carlisle.

Dogs get a mention. Small dogs were charged at one-quarter of the adult fare. But there was special treatment for working sheep dogs, which were carried free. There were complex rules about parcels and goods including a note stating: "Parcels containing urgent medicines are accepted for conveyance on Sundays." The idea that a bus was the best form of transport for urgent medicines seems quaint, to say the least.

Preston Corporation Transport Department, June 1970
28 pages, 215x140mm. Price 6d.

Preston's modern bus station opened in 1969, and featured on the cover of Preston's 1970 timetable with buses which looked curiously like Ribble's Atlantean coaches, with their translucent rear lower-deck windows. It was, the cover noted, an "Official timetable" – as if there were likely to be unofficial ones.

Inside it made partial use of the standard layout recommended by the British Omnibus Public Relations Committee, with the first page devoted to an explanation of the 24-hour clock: "Although it may take you a little time to get used to the 24-hour system it's really very simple." It then gave examples, before concluding: "You'll soon get the hang of it!"

It also warns of an impending change which was going to be rather more important than the 24-hour clock: decimalisation of Britain's currency from 15 February 1971. It encouraged readers to "make a good start by getting to know the new coins" and showed the six which were to be introduced.

Preston at this time used route letters rather than numbers, some of which related to the outer terminus – for example FP for Farringdon Park, GL for Gamull Lane. The only advertising in Preston's bus timetable was for other municipal departments – the baths and libraries.

London Transport Route 167, July 1971
12 pages, 180x110mm. Free.

London Transport excelled in its publicity, and this gift-wrapped single-decker, marked "For you" is an idea way ahead of its time. Sadly, it was an unwanted gift, as passengers would soon be complaining about LT's new standee single-deckers, likening them to cattle trucks. The message on the cover explains the benefits of one-man operation adding: "More economical operating may save some routes from being withdrawn or severely reduced."

The 167 ran between Debden and Ilford every half hour, and there's a fare table which shows that adult fares ranged from 2.5p to 17.5p. Including a fare table was intended to encourage passengers to have the correct fare ready.

Green Line, July 1979
68 pages, 210x150mm. Price 20p.

The price of this timetable is surely a measure of 1970s inflation. Just over ten years earlier the chunky 212-page Leeds book cost 6d – 2.5p. The Green Line book cost almost ten times that. The cover featured a new Duple-bodied AEC Reliance, with in the background representations of St Paul's Cathedral, Big Ben and a concrete structure which must have been part of the South Bank complex.

The Green Line network was still extensive, with 30 routes listed, some of them very long. Guildford to

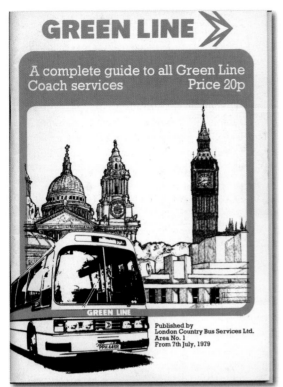

GREEN LINE ➤➤

A complete guide to all Green Line
Coach services   Price 20p

GREEN LINE

Published by
London Country Bus Services Ltd.
Area No. 1
From 7th July, 1979

Hertford took 3 hours 23 minutes; East Grinstead to Hemel Hempstead, 3 hours 29 minutes. Both routes ran hourly. The timetable advised that: "On Green Line coaches there are usually no short distance fares for journeys of less than 1 mile except inside the GLC area where there are no short distance fares for journeys of less than 2 miles."

Four pages of the timetable are devoted to places and events worth visiting by Green Line.

West Midlands Travel 966 coach timetable, July 1987
6 pages, 215x100mm. Free.

A nice image of a Time Saver MCW Metrobus appears on the front of this leaflet for the service between Wolverhampton and Birmingham International Airport. Although the 24-hour clock had been in widespread use in bus timetables for more than 20 years, WMT still felt it necessary to explain how it worked.

End to end journey time

TIMESAVER

966

WOLVERHAMPTON ▶ BIRMINGHAM
INTERNATIONAL AIRPORT

COACH
TIMETABLE
West Midlands Travel
SERVICES FROM 12 JULY 1987

was 1 hour 25 minutes, and the service ran every half hour. There is still a 966 serving the airport, but running between Erdington (which was on the 1987 route) and then carrying on to Solihull.

London Transport C1 Central Hoppa leaflet, August 1987
4 pages, 210x100mm. Free.

Hop on
the new
CENTRAL
hoppa

Route C1
Now extended to
Waterloo
Your frequent local bus service
from London Transport.
⊖BUS   Starts for August

An Optare CityPacer features on the front of this leaflet, heralding the bold new face of London's buses. It was issued to mark the extension of the C1 to run not just from Kensington to Westminster, but onwards to Waterloo. It ran every 6-7 minutes, six days a week, with a 50p flat fare.

Today's C1 is recognisably related to that of 25 years ago, starting further north at White City, but still running between Kensington and Westminster, although not to Waterloo. Today's buses are Alexander Dennis Enviro200s, operated by London United.

Reading Buses 328-331 leaflet, 1999
10 pages, 210x100mm. Free.

Optare was the bus industry style leader in the 1990s, and its Delta, based on a DAF SB220 chassis, was a suitably modern bus for the cover of this fold-out leaflet for services operated by Reading Buses between Reading and High Wycombe. The cover is hardly a model of clarity, but the bus photo and the route numbers are a clear enough description of what the leaflet is about.

There are just two notices for users. One is that there are no children's fares after 10pm (not 22.00 despite the

Time
TABLES
328
329
330
331
READING
HENLEY
MARLOW
HIGH WYCOMBE

For full information
about all our services
telephone direct on
0118 959 4000

READING Buses
GOING PLACES TOGETHER
Reading
BOROUGH COUNCIL

Head Office
Great Knollys Street
Reading RG1 7HH

Travel Shop
Duke Street
Reading RG1 4SA
0118 959 4000
(all departments)

ISSUE 1A/11/98

timetable using the 24-hour clock) and that if buses are delayed "the maximum claim payable is the bus fare for the delayed journey".
And not a word about dogs.

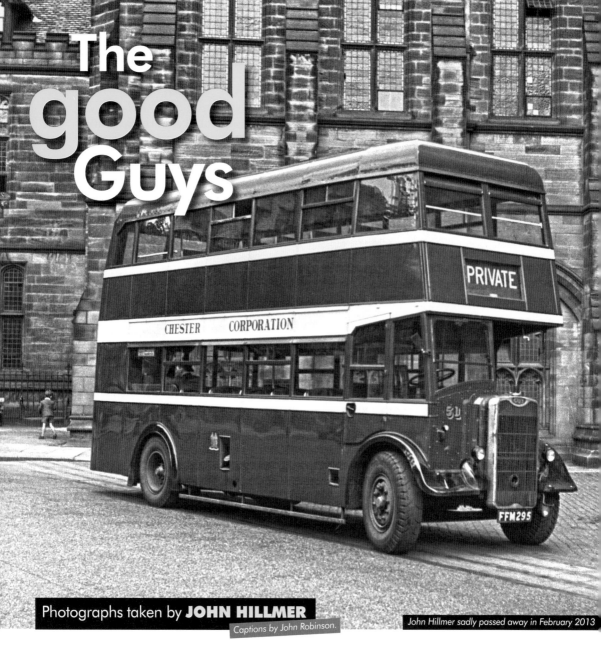

The good Guys

Photographs taken by **JOHN HILLMER**

Captions by John Robinson.

John Hillmer sadly passed away in February 2013

Arguably having the strongest character of all the wartime body styles was that produced by Massey Bros of Wigan, with its bold emphasis on angularity. Chester 51 was the first of a batch of five Arab II 5LWs, with Massey utility bodywork, new in 1944. Arab IIs had an extended bonnet irrespective of whether they had a 5LW or 6LW engine, although the position of the engine oil filler access holes in the bonnet side panel would generally indicate the engine type. With the shorter 5LW engine this was set back about 6in from the position used with the 6LW, where it was close behind the radiator. Three of the Guys were re-bodied in 1952 by Davies (two) and Massey (one). This bus survived in original condition and was withdrawn from passenger service in 1955, although it spent another four years as a training bus before being sold in 1959. It is seen parked out of service in St Werburgh Street, next to the city's fine cathedral, on 14 July 1952. Chester became a loyal Guy customer. It received its first Arabs in 1943 and continued to purchase them for its double-deck requirements until 1969, when it took delivery of the final three to be built for the UK market. In 1970, just before the first Daimler Fleetlines arrived, the Chester double-deck fleet was entirely Guy Arab.

LEFT: In 1943, Southdown started taking delivery of a batch of utility Guy Arabs that eventually totalled 100. It took three years to deliver them all, and four different body manufacturers were involved – East Lancs, Northern Counties, Park Royal and Weymann. This 1946 Northern Counties-bodied bus is strategically parked outside Bobby's Antiques and Furniture shop in Pevensey Road, Eastbourne (for which it carries an advert) in June 1952. The shop is behind the Fiat car. The official specification for wartime bodies was of wood-framed construction with no window pans, so the body framing itself formed the window pillars. However Northern Counties was allowed to continue using its metal-framed body design, complete with pressed window pans with rounded corners, for its utility bodies. Another Northern Counties feature was the radiused top corner to the cab offside window. By 1946, with the constraints of war now receding, the utility specification was relaxed allowing bodybuilders to inject some style into their designs again, of which this is a good example – elegant but not over-stated. A small step has been built into the front of the nearside mudguard to assist conductors in reaching the handle to turn the destination blind. Thirty-three of Southdown's utility Guy were converted to open-top configuration (32 for passenger work and one as a tree-lopper); many of these then served until the 1960s. This bus was one of several which passed to the Llandudno & Colwyn Bay Electric Railway in 1956, following its abandonment of trams and their replacement by Guy Arabs sourced from a number of operators. Bus operation was short-lived and the company sold out to Crosville in May 1961.

RIGHT: East Kent received 65 utility Guy Arabs between 1943 and 1945, with three Arab Is and 62 Arab IIs, forging a link with Guy Motors which continued until the final batch of Arabs IVs entered service in 1956/57. East Kent never used fleet numbers as it always managed to secure registrations containing numbers which did not duplicate existing ones. Consequently, all vehicles were referred to by the number in their registration. This is 255, the last of the three Arab I 5LWs, first licensed on 1 April 1943 and seen operating a city service in Canterbury in 1952. It was bodied by Park Royal, which had built the prototype utility body and went on to produce the highest number of utility bodies, and also built the biggest number of bodies on Guy Arab chassis. The Arab I had conventional mudguards as shown here and a normal-length bonnet unless fitted with the larger 6LW engine which required an extended bonnet, giving a pronounced 'snout' effect, together with the characteristic mudguards with upturned leading edge as used on Arab IIs. This bus lasted until 1958, the last year that East Kent ran utility Guys in their original form, though six were converted to open-top; five running until 1968 and one until 1969.

ABOVE: **Devon General took its first utility Guy Arab in 1943 and received three further batches up to 1945, as well as obtaining two second-hand from Rhondda that year, giving it a fleet of 26 Arabs with bodywork by Park Royal and Weymann. This bus, from the company's final batch of six Arab IIs with Park Royal bodies, is seen in Torquay operating service 12 Paignton. Tucked in behind is one of eight Weymann-bodied AEC Regent IIIs delivered between December 1946 and February 1947 and the company's first new postwar double-deckers. Devon General didn't purchase any more Guys, preferring AECs and Leylands, although 20 Arab IVs joined the fleet on 1 April 1970 when Exeter Corporation Transport was acquired.**

LEFT: **After the War Guy offered the option of a Meadows 6DC engine as an alternative to the Gardner 5LW or 6LW. Standing in Wetmore Road bus station, Burton upon Trent, in June 1953 is a Stevenson's Arab III with Massey bodywork, new in May 1949, on the operator's main service from Uttoxeter to Burton. This was a one-off, with a Meadows engine when new although it was converted to a Gardner 5LW some years later and lasted in the fleet until 1969. Based in Spath, just outside Uttoxeter, Stevenson's distinctive yellow and black livery was instantly recognisable. This was their second Guy Arab double-decker.**

During World War 2 Winchester became a reception area for war evacuees and extra buses were required to cope with the additional demand this created. This was recognised by the Ministry of War Transport allocating an 'unfrozen' Brush-bodied Leyland Titan TD7 to R. Chisnell & Sons, better known as King Alfred Motor Services, in March 1942. This was followed by four Guy Arab utilities; two Brush-bodied Arab Is in 1942, one Strachans-bodied Arab II in 1943 and one Weymann-bodied Arab II in 1944. All five buses had lowbridge bodywork. The final bus is seen in Winchester's Broadway on 20 June 1952 working out to South Wonston via Hookpit and the idyllically-named Stoke Charity. The body appears to be in original condition, with the obligatory single opening windows on each side of each deck, although the destination indicator has been rebuilt with radiused corners and flush-fitted glass. Weymann's utility bodywork could be readily-identified by the tall cab side windows, rising virtually to upper-deck floor level. The prominent external ribbing on the roof was another feature, although also present on Duple utility bodies.

Seen outside the Berresfords garage at Cheddleton in May 1985 is an Alexander-bodied Daimler Fleetline which had been new in 1972 to Sheffield Transport.

Three decades of change

Cliff Beeton tracks the fortunes of independent bus operators in North Staffordshire over the last 30 years.

At the start of the 1980s there were just five independents running in North Staffordshire – Stoniers, Berresfords, Procters, Turner's and Pooles Coachways – a far cry from the numerous operators running in the halcyon days of the 1950s. This was because the dominant local operator, Potteries Motor Traction, had adopted a vigorous policy of buying up small bus businesses in the area so that by the

1970s just these five remained. It is a measure of their strength that in 1980 all except Pooles were running double-deckers into Hanley Bus Station.

Local bus service deregulation in October 1986 enabled new operators both good and bad to dip their toes in the water and start running local buses. Some of these have stayed the course and become established players, others have been purchased by bigger groups, and a few have been unsuccessful and fallen by the wayside.

Berresfords/Stoniers

Berresfords Motors of Cheddleton had purchased Stoniers of Goldenhill in 1976 and since then the red and cream vehicles from the Berresfords fleet could be regularly be seen working Stoniers routes. Both had been running buses since the 1920s. A compulsory purchase order on the Goldenhill premises of Stoniers had seen them relocate to an old pottery factory site in Parsonage Street, Tunstall, in the early 1980s. In 1980 Berresfords was the only operator still running half-cab double-deckers in North Staffordshire, although these were soon to be replaced by rear-engined Leyland Atlanteans and Daimler Fleetlines.

Stoniers first rear-engined double-deckers were two four-year-old ex-Maidstone Atlanteans in 1977. Both fleets later received ex-Nottingham and West Yorkshire examples, alongside ex-Bournemouth and South Yorkshire PTE Daimler Fleetlines, as well as ex-London Country Green Line AEC Reliances and ex-Greater Manchester Transport AEC Swifts.

Both companies also operated joint services with PMT, Stoniers from Hanley to Bentilee, and Berresfords on the 16 between Hanley and Leek, which was also operated jointly with Procters. This joint operation would cease on deregulation.

Troubles with the Traffic Commissioners and issues with the Inland Revenue saw various vehicles hired from Lancashire United, Bournemouth Transport and Lancaster to keep services running at the start of the 1980s. Rumours in 1983 of the imminent demise of Berresfords saw PMT acquire second-hand Bristol REs from Bristol Omnibus to step in to operate the Berresfords services, but in the event this never happened.

Following the death of proprietor Jim Berresford both businesses were sold to PMT in April 1987. Initially both depots continued running under PMT ownership, but both were soon closed, after which only three ex-Berresfords vehicles survived in the PMT fleet, one former Trent Bristol RE and two Leyland Leopard coaches.

Turner's

Turner's of Brown Edge ran just one route, between Hanley, Smallthorne, Norton and Brown Edge, with an immaculate fleet of five Northern Counties-bodied Daimler Fleetlines in a traditional tudor maroon and deep cream livery with scroll fleetnames. The last of these was delivered in1980, and all were purchased new. A small fleet of coaches was also owned, these being painted green and cream.

The first second-hand rear-engined double-deckers to join the fleet did so in 1982 when two relatively young ex-London Transport DMS Daimler Fleetlines arrived from Ensign Bus, with the two oldest Fleetlines going in part exchange.

After deregulation Turner's concentrated on its traditional route but soon found that the Hanley to Smallthorne section was flooded with PMT minibuses operating from Biddulph and Chell into Hanley. Turner's passengers were always very loyal to them, so whether direct competition against them would have been successful for PMT is open to debate; nevertheless they sold out to PMT in October 1987.

The last vehicles to arrive some six months before the sale were two four-year-old Leyland Olympians with Roe bodywork, prematurely withdrawn by West Yorkshire PTE on the formation of Yorkshire Rider. These buses replaced the DMSs and were the first vehicles to carry route number blinds. Turner's allocated number 49 to its Hanley to Brown Edge service. In later years it became 69. At first PMT kept the Turner's garage in Brown Edge, but later closed it and moved the vehicles to its Clough Street garage in Hanley. However such was passenger loyalty that PMT kept the Turner's livery until the arrival of the FirstBus corporate identity in the late 1990s.

Procters

Procters of Fenton is the only remaining pre-deregulation independent operator still operating in North Staffordshire. Indeed by 2013 it had been

Stoniers operated this ex-Greater Manchester PTE Seddon midibus. It is seen at Mow Cop on a chilly day in January 1985.

The only low-floor Dennis Dart in the Procters fleet is this ex-Trent Barton bus with Plaxton Pointer body, seen here at Fenton in 2009.

operating route 16 from Hanley to Leek via Cheddleton for 90 years. In the early 1980s Procters had four double-deckers, two Daimler Fleetlines and two Leyland Atlanteans, all with Alexander bodywork and all purchased new. A second-hand purchase in 1982 was an ex-Tayside Bristol VRT with Alexander bodywork. This operated in Tayside two-tone blue and white, with Procters fleet names. This was subsequently adopted as fleet livery.

A change of direction in 1979 had seen Leyland Leopard coaches with Plaxton Supreme bodywork to bus grant specification arrive. These were used on route 16 as well as private hire and school work. The last double-deckers were withdrawn in December 1988. These Leopards were long-lasting with Procters, completing over 20 years service, their successors being second-hand Fiat/Carlyle minibuses, these later being replaced by MCW Metroriders from Northern General.

The first rear-engined single-deck bus was an ex-London MAN with Marshall bodywork which did not last long. The current standard is the Dennis Dart with Plaxton Pointer bodywork of which there are four in the fleet, including an ex-Trent low-floor example.

In September 2008 Procters won route 70 between Stoke and Bentilee under contract to Stoke-on-Trent City Council, which allocated a Cityrider-liveried

Optare Solo to work the route. It also worked on route 16 at times, where in 2009 some peak-hour journeys were extended via Stoke Station to Newcastle Bus Station. Route 70 was withdrawn in May 2011. The livery has evolved over the years from blue and cream to be mainly white with orange with blue fleet names.

Pooles

Pooles Coachways of Alsagers Bank had been operating since 1925 and ran mainly Leyland Leopard service buses, many purchased new, in an ivory and maroon livery into Newcastle from the surrounding villages of Knutton, Silverdale, Alsagers Bank, Audley and Park Site as well as colliery services and works buses to Rists wires and cables factory.

Before his death Jim Berresford, the owner of Berresfords Motors, was in the process of purchasing Pooles and even loaned them an ex-London Country RP-class AEC Reliance and an ex-Lothian Seddon mini. But the paperwork was never signed and Pooles was eventually sold to haulage contractors G&B McCready. Under McCready ownership a blue and white livery was introduced, and the fleet name was changed to Pooles Travel. Gradually the Leopards were replaced by Leyland Nationals and coaches. The bus services were eventually sold to PMT, but none of the vehicles ever operated with PMT.

Stevensons operated this Wadham Stringer-bodied Leyland Swift from its Burslem Garage. It is seen at Chesterton in June 1995.

This Seddon Pennine with Alexander Y-type bodywork was part of the Handy Bus fleet, but when photographed in Ball Green in 1996 was running for Knotty Bus and Coach. It had been new to Eastern Scottish in 1978.

This Knotty Bus Marshall-bodied AEC Swift had been new to Blackpool Transport and was photographed in Longton in 1994. It was destroyed in the 1998 garage fire.

D&G Coach and Bus ran some Optare Excels which had been new to sister company Choice Travel. One loads in Newcastle in October 2008.

Stevensons/Matthews

Stevensons of Uttoxeter gained a foothold in North Staffordshire when it purchased Crystal Coaches of Newcastle in 1983, initially running schools and works contracts. Expansion on deregulation led to it winning tendered work in Newcastle and the Potteries, and obtaining new premises on an industrial estate in Burslem. Interesting additions to the fleet in 1992 were a couple of the rare ex-South Yorkshire PTE Optare-bodied Dennis Domino midibuses. The fleet by 1995 was mainly Mercedes minibuses with a couple of Leyland Swifts.

Stevensons was later purchased by British Bus, which also owned Midland Red North and which had a depot at Etruria. These operations were then transferred to Burslem. Arriva, the successor to British Bus, later decided to sell the Burslem operations to Matthews Motors, reviving the former Crystal Coaches name. Most of the vehicles passing to Matthews Motors were surplus Midland Red North Iveco minibuses transferred in from Shrewsbury. A couple of Leyland Tigers with Duple Laser bodywork were also transferred.

Matthews Motors had been started by Jimmy Matthews after deregulation, mostly operating tendered work, but also running commercially on the Knutton to Newcastle and Hanley routes using second-hand Ford Transits in a pale blue and maroon livery. The fleet name later changed to Handy Bus. When Pooles Coachways sold its bus services to PMT, Handy Bus acquired Pooles' coaching business. Larger buses, including two Bristol LH/ECW buses and an Alexander-bodied Seddon later joined the fleet.

Following the purchase of the Crystal Coaches operation from Arriva, Matthews Motors later closed the Burslem depot, moving all the operations to Chesterton. Continuing issues with the Traffic Commissioners eventually led to the demise of Handy Bus and its associated companies.

Knotty

Knotty Bus and Coach was started in 1988 with a strong allegiance to AEC products. The livery was loosely based on the pre-Stagecoach Western Scottish black, grey, red and white, although every vehicle had each colour applied in different proportions. Initial commercial services operated were route 1, from Norton Estate via Burslem to Hanley; route 2, Chell Heath to Burslem and Hanley, and route 8 from Hanley to Biddulph Moor. Tendered services took the buses to Stone via Longton and Chesterton. Private hire and school contracts were also operated.

Pooles Coachways' last new vehicle was this Leyland Leopard with Marshall bodywork, seen in Ironmarket, Newcastle in 1985.

Classic vehicles like ex-Blackpool, London Country and St Helens AEC Swifts, a London Country RP-class AEC Reliance with Park Royal bodywork and a solitary ex-Blackpool Marshall Camair-bodied Dennis Lancet ran the local services. Sadly some of these were destroyed by a fire at the Chesterton garage in 1998. The business was sold in 1998 and ceased shortly afterwards

Scragg's

Scragg's of Bucknall, a taxi operator, started running buses after deregulation using the Blue Bus fleetname. Initial routes were Hanley to Abbey Hulton and Hanley to Ball Green using Freight Rover Sherpas in a mid-blue livery with yellow fleetnames. Over the years these were replaced with Mercedes-Benz minibuses. Scragg's ran some Optare Solos for a short while but found them thirsty when it came to fuel so they didn't last too long.

When PMT acquired the routes and vehicles of Moorland Rover of Weston Coyney, Scragg's stepped in and registered identical routes between Werrington, Weston Coyney and Newcastle operating as Moorland

Buses with similar vehicles in a similar livery. The Newcastle to Werrington route still operates today along with the Hanley to Abbey Hulton service. Some buses ran in the company's brown, yellow and cream coach livery.

An ex-Scottish Leyland Olympian joined the fleet in 2009 primarily for schools but also works a Leek to Hanley journey on route 16 and was followed by the first Plaxton Primo, with another five being added by the end of 2012.

A new garage at Adderley Green is in the process of being commissioned in 2013; the old premises in Bucknall are now too small.

D&G

D&G Coach and Bus was established in 1998 by David Reeves and Gerald Henderson primarily to operate tendered bus services. Initially the livery was plain mid blue but this was soon changed to incorporate cream relief. Originally based at the old PMT Longton bus station, and operating mainly second-hand Mercedes minibuses, gradual expansion introduced Optare Solos and Dennis Darts with bodywork from various

Scragg's operates six Plaxton Primos. One is seen at Abbey Hulton in 2011.

bodybuilders into the fleet, which eventually became the largest in the area after First Potteries.

In 2001 Stoke-on-Trent City Council introduced a policy of purchasing new vehicles under the Cityrider scheme to hire to bus operators winning successful tenders. This was to ensure modern low-floor buses would be used on non-commercial routes. D&G took delivery of the first three Cityrider-liveried Dennis Darts in February 2002 and went on to run a sizeable fleet of Cityrider Darts and Optare Solos.

Following the reduction of the First Potteries operator's licence in 2004 D&G won a temporary contract for three school services which required double-deckers. Three ex-West Midlands Travel MCW Metrobuses were hired for these services and were to be the only double-deckers ever operated by D&G in North Staffordshire.

A new purpose-built depot was opened at Mossfield Road in Adderley Green, (and also another at Crewe in Cheshire) to operate tendered services won from Arriva. A two-tone red livery was introduced to replace the blue and cream livery in 2008. A Wright-bodied Volvo B10B was painted in a two-tone green

livery with 118 Buxton Flyer fleetnames for route 118, Hanley to Buxton, that had been won from First PMT, and it even received fleet number 118. It only lasted a year on this route and was replaced by a former Alton Towers Transport Optare Tempo which received the same livery. In 2010 D&G took over the RML Travel routes and vehicles (except for the RML-class Routemaster which gave the business its name) following the collapse of that operator.

The end of D&G as an independent in North Staffordshire came in August 2011 when the business was purchased by Arriva and merged with Arriva-owned Wardle Transport. The D&G operations at Crewe were not part of the sale, so D&G vehicles could still be seen in Newcastle on service 85 to Crewe. In February 2012 the 85 was extended to Hanley bringing D&G vehicles back to the Potteries.

Copeland's

Copeland's of Meir is a long-established Stoke-on-Trent coach operator which began operating buses on route 40 connecting Longton, Blurton, Heron Cross and Fenton in 1989. At first Mercedes-Benz minibuses with

ABOVE: **Many of the buses and coaches in the Bakers fleet carry personalised registrations. Alexander ALX200-bodied Volvo B6LE 5777 RU was new to Stagecoach Manchester in 1997 as P344 JND and is seen in Biddulph in 2009.**

BELOW: **Copeland's operated two former PMT Dennis Darts on route 40, the Longton-Fenton circular. Lady Deborah looks very smart in Hollybush Estate in 2010.**

Bakers most modern buses are three Volvo B5H hybrids with Wrightbus bodywork and they wear a green and yellow version of the fleet livery which promotes them as "the only clean and green buses in Staffordshire". One is seen at Bradeley in May 2012.

Reeve Burgess bodywork were used, but latterly the Dennis Dart with Plaxton Pointer body was favoured. Two immaculate blue-liveried examples in the fleet are named Lady Sarah III and Lady Deborah, and are unusual examples of former FirstBus vehicles being sold for further service. They had been new to First PMT in 1990 for its Crosville operations. In 2009 Copeland's expanded its bus operations by winning the Council contract for Sunday operation on route 16, Hanley to Leek, The route stayed with Copeland's for 12 months before passing to Scragg's of Bucknall in 2010.

Bakers

Bakers of Biddulph is another long-established coach operator that has expanded into buses in a big way since deregulation. Today it has more buses than coaches in its fleet, and also possesses the most modern fleet in North Staffordshire including Wright StreetLites and Enviro200Darts. The company's coaches are green and white, while its buses are in a blue and yellow livery.

Taking advantage of Arriva Midlands' withdrawal in South Cheshire, Bakers started operating the main Biddulph to Congleton route. Expansion into the Potteries then followed with route 9, Biddulph to Hanley via Chell Heath. This gave the residents of Chell Heath a direct service into Hanley.

First Potteries introduced competing services, but the route proved so popular that larger vehicles are now used by Bakers.

When First Potteries had its operator's licence reduced in 2004, Bakers took over route 33, Newcastle to Westlands. New route 94, Biddulph to Newcastle, was introduced at the same time to provide positioning journeys to Newcastle for the 33. Initially just a few trips a day were provided on route 94, but they became very successful due to reliability problems with PMTs Biddulph to Newcastle buses. Passengers asked Bakers to put on more journeys which they did. Today the route runs every half hour during the day.

Route X1, Hanley to Stafford via Beaconside, was introduced in 2004 with three brand new Wright Cadet-bodied DAFs for students at Staffordshire University and as a rail replacement bus on behalf of Central Trains for the closed Wedgwood and Barlaston stations. So successful was the X1 that Bakers applied for and won a £300,000 government Green Bus Fund grant in 2010 for three hybrid double-deckers to replace the overcrowded Cadets on this service. Demonstration vehicles from both Alexander Dennis and Wrights were tried in service before the Wright-bodied Volvo B5H was chosen.

These entered service in October 2011 in a green and yellow version of Bakers' livery. Further modern vehicles introduced in 2012 were seven second-hand Wright StreetLites for new service X75 linking Hanley to Keele University, and local services to Knutton and Park Site estates from Newcastle.

Wardle

Wardle Transport operated its first service buses in 2002, using three Stoke-on-Trent City Council-owned Optare Aleros in Cityrider colours on routes 898 and 899 linking Brown Edge and Norton to Haywood Hospital and Burslem. The reduction in the PMT operator's licence led to Wardle winning the permanent contract to operate some school contracts that D&G had been operating temporarily. Three ex-Hong Kong tri-axle Leyland Olympians were added to the fleet, each painted in different all-over adverts for Wardle Travel, an associate company.

Further retrenchment by PMT saw Wardle introduce route 62, running between Hanley, Norton, Ball Green, Haywood Hospital and Burslem, partly commercial and partly replacing the 898 and 899. To operate these services four Cityrider Dennis Darts were transferred from D&G and painted into a new Wardle red and white livery. Wardle was also successful in winning

City Council tenders, mainly at the expense of D&G, so the fleet of Council-owned buses also grew to include Darts, Solos and Optare Versas, one of which was in a plum and silver livery with leather seats and laminate flooring for the Plumline service linking Hanley to Trentham Lakes and Blurton.

A contract to supply Stoke City Football Club with double-deckers for a shuttle service from Stoke to the Britannia Stadium on match days eventually provided work for six buses, and with registered bus services from Newcastle, Hanley and Smalthorne to the football ground, coupled with transport from Stoke Station for away fans, up to 13 vehicles could be utilised. Double-deckers joining the fleet included Leyland Olympians new to Merseyside PTE and Nottingham, as well as four ex-Stagecoach London Dennis Tridents, giving Wardle a larger double-deck fleet than First PMT.

Wardle ceased to be an independent operator when it was sold to Arriva Midlands in August 2010 but continued to run as a separate unit with a red and maroon version of the Arriva livery.

RML Travel

RML Travel commenced operations on 2 September 2006, with commercial route 40, Hanley to Birches Head, operating on a 20 minute headway during the

Seen at Burslem in 2008 is a Wardle Transport Volvo Olympian with East Lancs Pyoneer body. It started life with Nottingham City Transport ten years earlier as R468 RRA.

The first open-platform bus to work in service in the Potteries for many years was this RML Travel Routemaster, seen in Birches Head in September 2009 complete with a full set of blinds for route 40. It started life as a London Transport Country Area bus in green livery.

One of the Optare Versas owned by Stoke-on-Trent City Council is seen running in Burslem in 2008 for Wardle Transport with apt registration WT08 BUS.

day, Monday to Saturday. This circular route only required one vehicle so on the first day of operations the company's Routemaster, former Country Area RML2327, albeit now repainted red, worked the route. This was the first open-platform half-cab double-decker to operate a stage carriage service in the Potteries for more than 25 years.

The regular vehicle for the service was to be the unique Zig Zag rebuilt Dennis Dart, named Ziggy, which had been new to the Isle of Man and had a Carlyle body which had been extensively rebuilt by John Worker Systems with a view to prolonging the life of the vehicle. A second route, 41 Birches Head to Stoke and Newcastle, commenced the following year. An interesting acquisition was an ex-PMT Mercedes-Benz 811D with PMT-built Ami bodywork, which was appropriately named Amy. The Ami joined an assortment of second-hand Dennis Darts, Volvo B6s, Optare MetroRiders and latterly Mercedes minibuses working the routes.

RML Travel started the first night bus service in the Potteries in February 2008 with a flat fare of £2 and operating on Friday and Saturday nights, with a Monday night only N25 to Keele University for the benefit of students. Although encouraging, passenger loadings were not sufficient to continue the service. One exception was the night bus N64 from Market Drayton into Hanley that became so successful that a Leyland Lynx was needed to cope with the loadings.

RML started to experience difficulties in January 2010, with services ceasing to operate. D&G took over the buses, staff and routes, apart from the Routemaster.

The Eastern edge

DAVID LONGBOTTOM illustrates some of the vehicles to be found in the varied fleet of East Yorkshire Motor Services in 2012.

The Mercedes-Benz-based Optare Prisma was produced between 1995 and 1998, and East Yorkshire took 16 of the 122 built. A 1997 bus passes through Buckton on the Bridlington to Bempton service with a coach hire advert across the top of the windscreen.

A Volvo B7RLE with Wright Eclipse Urban body wears Wicstun Express livery, based on the traditional EYMS colours of indigo blue and primrose. The X4 Wicstun Express runs between Brough, Market Weighton and York. This Volvo, which was new in 2006, is heading south through Sancton. Wicstun is an old name for Market Weighton.

One of eight Alexander Dennis Enviro200s dating from 2007 that have always operated from Scarborough depot is seen loading for Eastfield outside the town's Victorian railway station. It carries Scarborough & District fleetnames.

This 2010 Volvo B7RLE with Wright Eclipse body is one of a pair that were delivered in Petuaria Express livery, once again based on traditional EYMS colours. The location is South Cave Market Place. Petuaria was a Roman fort at what is now Brough.

There are four Optare Solos in the East Yorkshire fleet, all of which came from the EYMS Group's Whittle subsidiary in Worcestershire. The oldest of these was new in 2001 and is the regular bus on the Elloughton and Brough local service. The Solos are 8.5m-long 29-seaters.

ABOVE: **There are six Plaxton Primos dating from 2006 in the East Yorkshire fleet, which have always been evenly split between the company's Hull and Bridlington depots. A Bridlington bus is on the summer Sunday and Bank Holiday Headlander route around the Flamborough Head area. It is leaving Bempton Cliffs RSPB reserve with the North Sea in the background.**

RIGHT: **Another Scarborough & District bus, a Plaxton Mini Pointer Dart leaving an autumnal Hunmanby for Scarborough on the service from Filey. New in 2000, this bus carries an East Yorkshire Motor Services 'EYM' registration.**

ABOVE: **Six Plaxton Centro-bodied Volvo B7RLEs joined the Scarborough fleet for park-and-ride duties in 2009. Two lost most of their park-and-ride branding in the autumn of 2012 following a reduction in the park-and-ride vehicle requirement. One of these heads for Filey on service X20 passing through the Blue Dolphin Holiday Camp.**

For a time the Northern Counties-bodied Volvo Olympian was the preferred vehicle at EYMS. Although usually confined to schools or works duties, this one is seen on Scarborough's South Cliff whilst working the service from Scarborough to Cayton. This bus was bought new in 1998 but the company also had similar vehicles acquired second-hand.

ABOVE: **A major change to the EYMS Group fleet in 2012 came with the acquisition of 27 former Go-Ahead London Plaxton President-bodied Volvo B7TLs. Five were converted to open-top for operation in Scarborough, four went to Finglands in Manchester, and the remaining 18 joined the main East Yorkshire fleet. One leaves Little Weighton on service 161 from Hull's Wyke College to Cherry Burton.**

BELOW: **The ex-London B7TL open-toppers in Scarborough replaced Volvo Citybuses on the seafront service. One waits at the Spa terminus at Scarborough's South Bay overlooking the sands with the background dominated by the Victorian Grand Hotel. When built in 1867 it was one of the biggest hotels in the world.**

The most common double-deck type in the East Yorkshire fleet is the Wright Eclipse Gemini on Volvo B7TL, and later B9TL, chassis. A B7TL dating from 2005 is seen passing through Barmston on service from Bridlington to Hornsea. It is a long-wheelbase 74-seater.

There are ten Alexander Dennis Enviro400H hybrids in use in Hull. This one is in Queens Dock Avenue in the city centre, rounding the floral displays on Queens Gardens. The hybrids were new in 2011 and are 77-seaters.

THEN AGAIN ... ●●●

Peter Rowlands yearns for constancy in a continually changing bus world.

All photographs by the author.

This ex-Newcastle Leyland Titan PD2 was repainted in original 1940s blue livery for the Jubilee celebrations in 1977. It is seen here at Gosforth Park.

Before I was born, the city buses in Newcastle were dark blue. I'm willing to believe this because I've seen pictures of them, and even some remarkable colour film taken in 1948. There it was: a familiar landscape, but one teaming with buses painted the wrong colour – an alternative version of the reality I grew up with.

But part of my brain refuses to believe this. As far as I'm concerned, buses in Newcastle were always yellow. (Another part of my brain thinks they still are, but let's not go there.) I have a sneaking suspicion that this kind of experience is shared by all who love the bus industry, forming part of a perpetual cycle in our perception of the rightness of things.

Phase 1 is the way things are when you first start noticing them. If it's the 1950s, it's front-engined buses. If it's the sixties, it's front engines on the way out, rear engines on the way in. If it's the seventies,

it's PTEs, National Bus Company and Leyland's last gasp. Whatever and whenever it is, it's the benchmark as far as you're concerned. It's simply how things should be.

Phase 2 is the big change. It's when you've got bored with what you were born to, and luckily so has the bus industry. So it waves a magic wand and makes everything exciting and new. New bus models, different body styles, new liveries. Out with municipal bus operations, in with company ownership and deregulation.

Phase 3 is the next episode. Further new liveries; new corporate identity (hello Stagecoach, Arriva, First, goodbye constituent colour schemes). It's all rather fine in its way. The industry is shaking itself out. It's moving with the times.

Phase 4 is when things start getting complicated. Yet more new liveries. Foreign ownership of bus operators (Transdev, Veolia, ComfortDelGro). Bus companies swapped between owners. Closures. Upheaval in the bus building world. Old favourites like MCW, Northern Counties and East Lancs now gone. Instead, ADL, Polish Scanias, Egyptian Darts.

Depending on your age, you might have to renumber my examples. My phase 4 might be your phase 2. But the other phases will come, trust me.

And when they do, suddenly you'll be thinking hang on, how many of these changes are we supposed to take in our stride? That's when nostalgia kicks in. Maybe that first phase wasn't so bad after all. Distant memories acquire a kind of glow. Can't we get back to those nicely ordered days? Sadly no; you'd have to unwind all that's happened since, and it ain't gonna happen.

Which is why, as an aside, commemorative bus liveries have such a bitter-sweet quality. They do, I'll grant you, give you a tantalising chance to experience a livery that maybe you never saw at the time, or that you remember fondly from childhood; but often you're shown it on a bus that hadn't even been thought of when the livery was current.

Worse, these revived liveries seem like a reproach. "See, this is what you once had," the operator seems to be saying, "but if you're imagining that we're going to paint the whole fleet like this, dream on. We've moved forward; why haven't you?"

If you're a part-time bus photographer (like most of us), the experience of the enthusiast's lifecycle is played out again and again. We can't be everywhere at once, much as we might like to be, so every time we visit a distant location, we have to adjust to change.

ABOVE: **Newcastle as the author will always remember it: yellow buses. In 1986 this Alexander-bodied Atlantean had just been repainted in Busways livery, but did not yet carry any fleetname.**

BELOW: **A MAN with Alexander ALX300 bodywork in Stagecoach's standard livery passes Fenwick's in Newcastle in May 2008. No yellow here now.**

Take Derby, for instance, which I first visited in the mid-1970s. It had a nice blue and grey city transport fleet then, and it was still running some open-platform double-deckers. So that was my baseline. Next time I was there the open-platform Daimlers were gone, but a crisper version of the livery had come in. Fine. Then what? Then came the remarkably colourful yellow, red and blue City Rider fleet. Even better in my book.

Then it was all gone. Swallowed up by what became Arriva.

Something rather similar happened in Bristol. Back in the seventies, I discovered a world still populated by dozens of front-engined Bristol Lodekkas. But gradually they dwindled, and before long they'd gone.

However, with privatisation came a new yellow, red and blue City Line livery – not unlike Derby's as it happens, but even more wacky. It was emphatic and confident, and I basked in its exuberance. This was the best kind of phase 3.

Then it was gone. Swallowed up by what became First.

ABOVE: **Still in service in Bristol in 1982, this NBC green 1967 Bristol FLF.**

BELOW: **Bristol City Line's exuberant red, yellow and blue livery is seen to good effect on this Leyland Lynx, descending from Clifton in 1996.**

But let's not be deceived here. Derby city buses weren't always blue and grey; that was just my personal benchmark. Previously they were green and cream; I just didn't ever see them in that colour scheme. Likewise the Bristol Omnibus livery wasn't always green; as it happens, it was previously blue.

How about Cambridge? The city of my childhood holidays had vivid Tilling red Bristol buses belonging to Eastern Counties. But by the time I started photographing them they were in NBC red. Then came Cambus and its extraordinary pale blue colour scheme, later gaining darker blue relief.

Then it was gone. Hello Stagecoach, hello stripes. Which was your benchmark here?

The Birmingham area, my home for three years when I was first working, unveiled a panoply of bus types I'd never encountered before – open-platform tin-fronted Daimlers and Guys, own-brand Midland Red D9s. But here was a paradox: when I arrived, West Midlands Passenger Transport Executive had just absorbed a whole bunch of municipal bus operations. The subtly different buses of each component part were still around, but with their

ABOVE: **Seen in 1977 in the centre of Cambridge, this 1967 Bristol RE with the early rounded style of ECW bodywork wears NBC red livery.**

BELOW: **In the mid-1990s, Cambus, the successor to Eastern Counties in Cambridge, had introduced this strange, insubstantial light blue livery, demonstrated here by an early flat-fronted Bristol VRT.**

dark blue and cream colour scheme they were all trying to look the same.

So what was my benchmark here? The new unified status quo, or the one I could see was quickly disappearing?

Well, I have to tell you that instead of resolving this massively important issue, I spent my time inwardly fuming over the fact that although the many Daimler Fleetlines looked quite like the Leyland Atlanteans from my home city, they didn't look similar *enough*. The canted rear domes of their Park Royal bodies lacked the upright dignity of the MCW bodies they resembled. According to me, that is.

Tush. I imported my own benchmark instead of finding one locally.

When I returned, the severe dark blue (much beloved of Birmingham Corporation fans, of course) had been replaced by a brighter, more cheery shade. This seemed a great improvement to me, though probably not to locals. Then I blinked, and that livery in turn had given place to a striking silver-based scheme. And then, under West Midlands Travel, an entirely new look came in, with a welcome if limited reinvention of local identities – harking back, in fact, to an era before I even set foot in the place.

Liverpool was much less of a challenge. As far as I was concerned, this was the land of green buses. Again, though, I couldn't help noticing the local variations in the PTE's bus fleets – AEC Swifts in St Helens, for instance. But it was only when I spotted the occasional trainer or retired bus in an older livery that I was aware of what had been lost.

After that, of course, the livery turned deep red and cream, and then disappeared altogether.

And Manchester: forever orange (though it wasn't, of course; it was previously red). But on my first visit, the variety of vehicles from the twelve municipal operations that made up Greater Manchester PTE fleet was striking, and it wasn't lost on me that they must all once have had their own distinctive identities. What I saw was Northern Counties bodies trying to look like Roes; Massey bodies, when I thought this make had disappeared; and giant, stately Mancunian double-deckers, unlike anything anywhere else (but out of production by the time I discovered them).

The orange survived into privatisation, but not for very long. In came the Stagecoach and First corporate look.

Then there was the land of my fathers. The Welsh valleys, on my first visit, had half a dozen council-run bus operations – some of them tiny. I missed

FAR LEFT: **Although Manchester's Mancunians wore a red and cream livery when the type was introduced, in their middle years they carried the orange Selnec/Greater Manchester PTE scheme. This Roe-bodied Daimler Fleetline is seen in Piccadilly Gardens in August 1981.**

LEFT: **One of Lincoln's Alexander-bodied Bristol VRTs in its green and cream livery in 1985. It had been new to Tayside Regional Transport.**

BELOW: **A West Midlands Travel Mercedes-Benz in central Birmingham July 2000.**

ABOVE: **An ex-London Transport Daimler Fleetline with Park Royal bodywork, seen in Grimsby Cleethorpes' brown livery in 1990.**

BELOW: **In 1987 Grimsby Cleethorpes Transport introduced an orange livery, seen here on an Alexander-bodied Leyland Tiger delivered at the end of that year.**

Merthyr's deep red double-deckers, but at least there were orange single-deckers. But one by one, those businesses were sold off. Now there are none.

This whole saga is played out endlessly. Nottingham buses are green (no they're not – they're a whole variety of colours). Darlington buses are dark blue (no they're not – that fleet was run out of town). Northampton buses are red (no they're not – the council fleet was sold off years ago). Lincoln buses are green; no, a different two-tone green; no, green and yellow; no, taken over by Stagecoach. Grimsby buses are brown; sorry, orange; sorry, gone.

But sometimes the spirit of the past survives. Take Brighton. Back in the 1970s it had a nice blue and grey council fleet, running alongside Southdown buses. This was my base position. However, before that, Brighton Hove & District had been the main company operator, and for a time the BH&D and council-run buses shared a predominantly red livery.

Later, when privatisation kicked in, Brighton & Hove was reinvented, and it's still with us today. It absorbed the municipal fleet, but the good news is that those nice people at Go Ahead, its parent company, have kept faith with the spirit of the old red and cream colours.

Then there's London. What can I say? Routemasters were my baseline when I moved here in the 1970s, and they were still here 30 years later, undermining my conviction that life means constant change. But where are the Fleetlines that were arriving when I did? Those were my benchmark too. Where are the Merlin single-deckers? Where are the Titans, the Metropolitans, the Metrobuses? Gone, and not coming back.

Southampton was in the throes of change in 1998. The CityBus red livery was still in evidence, as seen on this East Lancs-bodied Leyland Atlantean, but was being replaced by First's new corporate colours.

Yet London's livery has survived surprisingly unchanged. In fact as I write this, there's a definite retro look to its colour scheme (if you can call it a colour scheme). It had a drab all-over red phase in the 1970s, and lately all-over red has come back. The question now is whether to celebrate the continuity or deplore the minimalist incarnation of it. It's a tough call.

If your day was the day of NBC red and green, no doubt a part of you would love to see those colours make a reappearance. If it was the original Stagecoach stripes, maybe you're having trouble adjusting to the livery that replaced it. If it was First's Barbie Mk I, maybe you're struggling with Barbie Mk II and it's new lilac-based replacement. Everyone's baseline is different.

Instead of worrying about all those changes of detail, perhaps we should be celebrating the continuity of the big picture – the fact that we do still have a native UK bus manufacturing industry; we do still have some variety among operators and their identities (big groups, smaller groups, independents); and we even still have a few council-owned fleets.

Nothing in the bus industry will ever revert to the way it was when we first came to it. That needn't stop us celebrating what once was, but at the same time it shouldn't distract us from appreciating the best of what we still have.

I'm working on it.

Stagecoach bought the Grimsby Cleethorpes operation in 1993; its identity was replaced by anonymous Stagecoach stripes.

London pioneered the use of hybrid buses in Britain, and has the biggest fleet. The leading hybrid supplier in the UK is Alexander Dennis, and this Enviro400H was one of four delivered to Metroline at the end of 2008.

Advance
OF THE
hybrid

Hybrid buses may not yet be commonplace in Britain, but their numbers are growing. **RICHARD WALTER** illustrates a selection.

Volvo's main hybrid model is the B5LH with Wrightbus bodywork. Five were supplied to Arriva London in 2009. Wrightbus also build integral Gemini hybrids using VDL underframes. The green leaves motif was a feature of London's early hybrids.

Relatively few small operators run hybrids. This Volvo B5LH is one of four operated by Bullocks of Cheadle. It was new in 2011 and features the updated Gemini 2 style of Wrightbus body. All carry carefully-chosen registrations, this is BU11 OKS. The route-branding on the side notes that the bus produces 35% less CO2.

Greater Manchester has the biggest concentration of hybrids outside London with all three of the big groups – Arriva, First and Stagecoach – running various hybrid models. The Stagecoach buses are all Enviro400Hs and carry a distinctive green livery.

Transport for Greater Manchester has been a strong advocate of hybrids. Optare Versas supported by TfGM are used on a number of services in the region, as illustrated by a First Manchester bus on the service from Manchester to Swinton.

Another user of hybrid Versas is Black Diamond, part of Rotala. This 37-seater was new in 2012.

The biggest bus operator in the West Midlands, National Express, runs both Volvo, as seen here, and Alexander Dennis hybrids. Nine of each were delivered in 2011. The Volvos seat 68; the ADLs, 77. National Express uses a distinctive green livery with a "Turning Birmingham Green" message.

The supply of 15 Enviro400H hybrids to Lothian Buses in 2011 was a breakthrough for Alexander Dennis; Lothian's standard double-decker is the Volvo/Wrightbus combination. The company says the hybrids are 56% more fuel efficient than standard diesels.

The Scottish Government, like England's Department of Transport, has provided money to support the purchase of hybrid buses and most of these have, appropriately, been built in Scotland by Alexander Dennis. First Glasgow adopted a silver livery for its new Enviro400s on a cross-city service, although not all are in fact hybrids. First's double-deck hybrids in Manchester and Leeds are also silver.

Single-deck Volvo hybrids were delivered to First and to Lothian Buses in the spring of 2013. Lothian took ten of the 7900H model, which is a complete Volvo-built product. Lothian claims a capacity of 92 passengers – but just 34 get seats. Lothian perhaps underplays the environmental benefits of its hybrid fleet, with a gold-based livery and an 'eco' prefix to the fleetname.

You wait ages for a new hybrid bus then two turn up at once. Transport for London has ordered 600 of the Wrightbus-built New Bus for London, an idea dreamed up by mayor Boris Johnson in his search for a new Routemaster. The prototypes entered service with Arriva London in 2012, and two are seen here. The first production buses joined the Metroline fleet in the summer of 2013.

Now &then

The bus industry is constantly changing and adapting. Operators and manufacturers come and go. Routes are altered to meet changing travel patterns. And vehicle design is constantly evolving. **Geoff Mills** illustrates some of the changes in Colchester since he took his first bus photograph in 1953.

The very first G. R. Mills photograph in May 1953 shows a 1948 Bristol K5G in the Eastern National fleet. It is in St. John's Street bus park having worked in to Colchester from Brightlingsea via Wivenhoe at a time when the service, 78, was exclusively an Eastern National operation.

Cedric of Wivenhoe began operation from its base to Colchester as service 78X in October 1991, later extending through to Brightlingsea. When Eastern National withdrew from that section of the route Cedric became the sole operator. After Go-Ahead's acquisition of Hedingham Omnibuses in March 2012, the route was then contested from August 2012 by a Hedingham-operated 87 service. A Hedingham Alexander Dennis Enviro200, new in 2007, on the 87 leads a Cedric 1991 ex-Metrobus Olympian on the 78X in Colchester High Street in September 2012.

The second G. R. Mills photograph, also taken in St. John's Street bus park in May 1953, was this coach in the fleet of Osborne's of Tollesbury, a 1938 Bedford WTB with a 1949 Thurgood body. The original Plaxton body remained in Osborne's yard as a store shed for many years. The Bedford has worked in to Colchester from Tollesbury via Birch on service 2.

The Osborne's business was purchased by Hedingham Omnibuses in 1997 and service 2 was renumbered 92. This is a 2013 view of a 1998 Optare Excel loading for Tollesbury via Birch in Colchester's then newly-opened bus station, a line of stands in Osborne Street. The Excel was new to Bennetts of Gloucester and reached Hedingham Omnibuses via Konectbus of Dereham, which, like Hedingham, is another Go-Ahead business.

Blackwell of Earls Colne was a staunch Leyland supporter and had examples of various prewar Titan models on the Halstead – Earls Colne – Colchester service in the years after World War 2. The operations were sold to Hedingham Omnibuses in 1965. This 1932 TD2 had a second-hand Brush body which replaced the original Roe body fitted when the bus was supplied new to West Riding. The advert on the side, referring to the image of the bottle, says: "To read the label turn this bus on end. Guinness for strength." Pretty clever for 1956.

For several decades the timings on the service between Halstead and Colchester remained virtually unchanged. At the start of 2013 First Essex Buses (as the successor to former joint operator Eastern National) increased the frequency to hourly. A Northern Counties-bodied Leyland Olympian which had been new in to Yorkshire Rider waits in Osborne Street to take up its departure in March 2013 on a trip which extends beyond Halstead to Great Yeldham.

A 1936 Bristol JO5G in the Eastern National fleet waits in St. John's Street bus park in Colchester in July 1953, ready to take up a journey to Chelmsford. The 31-seat body was by Eastern Counties.

Offering a superior standard of comfort on the service between Colchester and Chelmsford in 2011 is this Scania OmniCity of First Essex Buses. It has 44 leather seats and air-conditioning. It is seen on Lexden Road in Colchester on service 71A which also serves Kelvedon and Witham.

A 1933 Leyland Titan TD2 with 1949 ECW body in the Eastern Counties fleet is seen in St. John's Street bus station in 1956 bound for Ipswich on the 207 service via Capel St. Mary. The bus was operated by Eastern Counties until 1961. Note the advert for Ilford films - "for faces and places".

In 2012 the service, now numbered 93, was operated by Carters of Capel St. Mary. An ex-London United Dennis Trident with Alexander ALX400 body loads in Queen Street bus station in Colchester, since closed.

Colchester Corporation's first diesel buses were five Massey-bodied AEC Regents delivered in 1939. One is seen at the Parsons Heath terminus of route 1 in 1953 where buses had to reverse. The Regent was withdrawn in 1957, while route 1 was extended in 1961 to serve the new Greenstead housing estate then under development.

Over five decades later the style of bus serving the Greenstead Estate via Parsons Heath has dramatically changed. Network Colchester is the successor to the former municipal bus operation, and this Scania N230 with Optare body is loading in Colchester High Street with route 1 branding – with the intermediate points listed on the side of the bus obscured by an advert.

Towards the end of their days with Colchester Corporation the fleet's two 1942 Bristol K5Gs with Bristol bodies were relegated to peak-hour duties. One is seen at Old Heath Post Office in 1953 on a short-working on service 6 from the town centre. It was withdrawn in 1956.

The same location in 2011, but with a vastly different bus. Under the ownership of TGM, Network Colchester frequently had vehicles on loan from associated operators. This 1999 Volvo B6 with Wright body is on loan from Arriva's Network Harlow operation, and the route branding is for that rather different Essex town. The destination shows that this really is a number 6.